Best Wishes

To Carolyn

Ian Stait

stark reality

stark reality

Three-times Badminton winner, European,
World and Olympic medallist

IAN STARK

with Jenny Stark and Kate Green

David & Charles

contents

page 2: My last ride on Murphy Himself, at the Barcelona Olympics
page 3: Receiving the Butler Challenge Bowl from HM the Queen at Badminton's 50th anniversary in 1999
left: Lady Hartington's 18hh The Moose, specially adorned with Scotland's emblem
pages 6–7: My first trip to Lexington in the USA, in 1998, where I was the sole Brit, and Saucy Brown finishes fourth

introduction

It only took one riding lesson at the age of ten to get me hooked. I had always fancied the idea of riding and my sister had lessons, but she became nervous and eventually handed over a lesson to me. After being led up and down the riding school drive with someone shouting 'Up down, up down', I was let loose for a ride. It was mind-blowingly terrifying and, at the same time, absolutely thrilling – and I couldn't wait to do it again.

The following Sunday I was out playing on Gala Hill outside Galashiels, where we lived, when some horses went past. I rushed home, conned ten bob out of my mother, who wasn't remotely horsey, and went back to the riding school where I waited four hours for my ride. Thereafter I spent a lot of time there, including when I should have been at school.

I begged, borrowed and stole rides off friends' ponies, joined the Duke of Buccleuch's branch of the Pony Club, and was doing gymkhanas and show jumping by the age of twelve, followed by my first Pony Club one-day event at the age of sixteen. A year later I first met my wife-to-be, Jenny McAulay, when we were in a team together.

I left school at eighteen and signed on at the dole office with no intention of looking for a job – and every intention of carrying on messing around with horses – but, to my horror, three days later the DHSS offered me a clerk's job in which, by some miracle, I stayed for the next ten years. Part of the job involved going to

top: A bit of fun at home
above: Debriefing with Robert Lemieux, Mark Todd and Hugh Thomas at Gatcombe in 1988

right: I come off best in a clash with Mark Phillips at Thirlestane in August 1988

people's homes and checking whether they were entitled to their social security benefits, but instead I would go off and ride and then tell the office later that they were out. Whenever Jenny asked me why I wasn't at work, I used to tell her airily that I was on 'flexi-time'!

With Jenny at the Horse of the Year Ball in 1993

below: *Time off at Atlanta*

I had an official hour's lunch break every day, during which I would exercise two horses, Greyfriars Bobby and Greyfriars Lass, riding one and leading the other. There was a ride around a hill that I could do in twenty minutes – provided I cantered the whole way and jumped the gates! Then I would rush home, throw their sweat rugs on and leave them with hay and water. Of course if someone did that with my horses now I'd be absolutely furious!

A friend, Jackie Rodger, and I used to buy horses jointly and sell them on and it was on one of those that I did my first BHS novice event, at the age of eighteen – over twenty-seven years ago! At the 1999 Europeans I suddenly realised that I had been eventing for longer than one of my team mates, Jeanette Brakewell, had been alive!

My first three-day event was the novice section at Wylye in 1978 with a horse called Woodside Dreamer who finished eighth. We were eighth in the Bramham novice three-day the following year and 11th in the standard section at Wylye.

Jenny and I drove down to Wylye that year in our old cattletruck and got hopelessly lost. The journey took about twelve hours and when we got Woodside Dreamer out of the lorry she was lame. I knew it was only a shoeing problem, so I worked her the next day and then trotted her up in front of the judges. They made me trot up eight times, by which time I was sweating and grey, and then said that I could do the dressage and that they would review the situation.

In the dressage every time I had to do 'big trot' I just kicked her into canter so she looked less lame. Needless to say, we didn't get a very good mark, but we were allowed to go across country, where we went clear, and she was perfectly sound.

above: *A scary ride on Desert Orchid at Windsor*

below: *The vet check at Badminton 1995 with Caliber*
right: *Winded after a crashing fall at the*
final team trial at Althorp in 1994

'Jenny and I slept in the cattle truck that weekend where things got quite "romantic"...'

Jenny and I slept in the cattle truck that weekend where things got quite 'romantic' and we decided there and then that we were going to get married and have babies as soon as possible. And so we did – we were married two months later, Stephanie was born within the year and, after another rather short gap, her brother Tim arrived. We moved into the home in which we still live, at Ashkirk, and I carried on riding novices and 'working'.

I had never liked my job and eventually it got to the point where I couldn't take much more. One morning just after Christmas 1982 I was reluctantly setting off for the office when I said to Jenny, who was mucking out, 'I really can't stand this any longer.' To my surprise she replied 'Well, leave then.' So I went straight into the office and handed in my notice, which everyone thought was a huge joke as I'd hardly been working there anyway!

'I was reluctantly setting off for the office when I said to Jenny, "I really can't stand this any longer." To my surprise she replied "Well, leave then" ...'

By this stage I had started riding Sir Wattie and Oxford Blue as youngsters, but I had no sponsor and the more time I spent concentrating on competing them, the less time I was spending on bringing on other horses and therefore making money. I was under serious pressure to sell Wattie and Robbie, but the Edinburgh Woollen Mill had stepped in earlier, which totally saved the day.

*top & above: Keeping cool at the Atlanta
Olympics in 1996*

*right: Riding Sir Marcus in the winning British
team at Chantilly in 1995 with Jemima Johnson
and Tiny Clapham*

The director David Stevenson and his wife Alix used the same accountant as me and were also members of our riding club. Both were leading athletes in their own right who had represented Britain – David was an international pole vaulter and Alix a long jumper – and they were also interested in racing, buying National

Hunt store horses and having horses in training, including Randolph Place, with whom I later had a shot at hunter chasing. David summoned a meeting and offered us sponsorship, which was to last for eight-and-a-half years. They set up a fund to buy the horses and my prize-money would go back into that fund, which meant that when the contract ended the horses were still mine.

Now, instead of a big sponsorship, I have twelve endorsement contracts. This sort of thing has tended to replace the big rider sponsorships and is a regular trend nowadays which I think we may have started. I also have two generous owners in Lady Hartington and Lady Vestey and I wouldn't ride for anyone else now.

We first met the Vesteys when after Gawler I realised that I needed a southern base for the spring advanced events and to prepare for the big three-days, as although there are many wonderful events in Scotland and the north of England, there just isn't the breadth of competition that you need before tackling Badminton. Henrietta Knight, who was chairman of selectors for Seoul, told me that her sister Ceci had a yard and cottage in Gloucestershire that we could use. I rang up what I

top: Lord Hartington in unusual pose!

above: The two 'ladies', who were both successful at Chatsworth, 1999: Lady Hartington (left) and Lady Vestey

later discovered was Lord Vestey's Stowell Park and asked to speak to Ceci, only for the butler to tell me crushingly, 'Her ladyship has just gone into dinner.' At this I panicked and rang Hen to ask, 'Who on earth *is* your sister?' But Ceci couldn't have been kinder.

The first time I arrived at Stowell Park it was in the dark, with a very full lorry and two exhausted, starving and totally over-awed children (who were due to start at a new school), Jenny having driven down separately from Scotland as there was no room for her. Ceci immediately took the children into the house and looked after them. We now stay in the big house, which is very spoiling, and it was there that we met their friends the Hartingtons.

It's a great arrangement with the two 'ladies' and we all get on very well. I realise how lucky I am always to have had sponsors and owners who are horsemen themselves and so understand what can go wrong with a horse. So often I have seen riders put under pressure from sponsors wanting a commercial

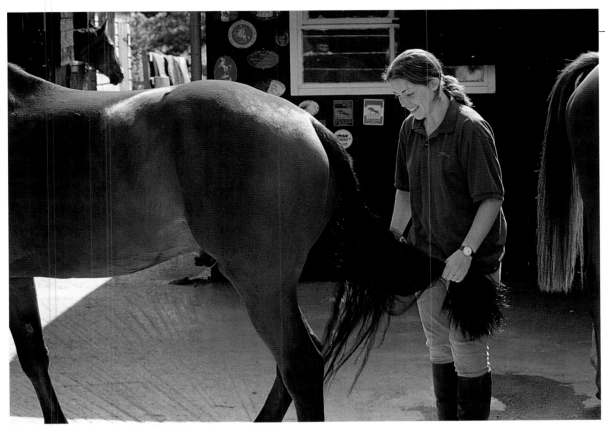

above: *Our daughter Stephanie at home*

result and not understanding where a horse is concerned how thin the line between success and failure can be.

Stephanie and Tim both had ponies, but Tim 'retired' somewhat abruptly at the age of eight – an age at which I hadn't even started riding! – after he and Stephanie had an argument about the rosettes he'd won! Stephanie kept it up much longer and was very successful as a Junior, representing Britain in the winning team in 1996 on Go Bust. But the pressure was very much on her, with commentators continually saying 'and here comes Ian Stark's daughter'. Eventually this became quite wearing and what with that and the awful experience of having a novice horse die after a fall, Stephanie also decided to 'retire' from the big time. She is now at Newcastle University and rides for fun.

The date of my own retirement isn't definite. I very much hope to get to the Sydney Olympics and, if all goes well, I could have five horses to choose from: Arakai, Jaybee, The Moose, Rangitoto and A Mouse Called Mickey. I try not to take chance rides any more or ride novices; I am only interested in concentrating at the bigger events now as, perhaps unusually for a rider approaching the end of an eventing career, I can honestly say that I have never had a better string of horses.

below: *Headgirl Vicky Welton with The Moose*

where it all began
Sir Wattie

The first time I sat on Sir Wattie was in my mother-in-law's indoor school when he was a four-year-old. I got on him and straight away he gave an enormous buck which almost had me up in the rafters. My mother-in-law was most impressed and said, 'Well, he'll either be brilliant or useless!'

I rode him on and off as a youngster for his owner-breeders Dame Jean Maxwell-Scott and Susan Luczyc-Wyhowska, but Wattie was a very difficult and time-consuming type of horse and it was hard to concentrate on him properly as I was still working for the DHSS then.

Wattie detested dressage and would have tantrums if you asked him to repeat something. He made terrible faces whenever he saw Barbara Slane-Fleming, who taught me dressage, and would get bored and stroppy. Because he was a quarter Welsh cob, the crosser he got, the more his knees would come up in the air in the action typical of that breed.

'Eventually Jenny said she absolutely had to go to the loo, but apparently I shouted, "No one move!"...'

above: Wattie as a foal with his mother, Rosa
opposite: My first Whitbread trophy in 1986
below: My first foreign three-day, Achselschwang in 1983

I remember working him in before the Los Angeles Olympics, where he was reserve horse, and all I wanted out of him was a 20-metre circle, but it was hours before he would do it. Jenny and Claire, our groom, were in the school with me in an atmosphere of desperate concentration. Eventually Jenny said she absolutely had to go to the loo, but apparently I shouted, 'No one move!'

Wattie came to me full-time as a five-year-old and after we'd been to one hunter trial, I decided he was ready for a horse trials! A year later I took him to Charterhall for his first intermediate, where he made one of the rare cross-country mistakes of his career. He jumped in too boldly into a coffin, got into difficulties and had to stop. But he was an incredibly bright horse and he never made this mistake again.

He was seven when I took him to his first three-day event, Bramham, in 1983, where he won the Standard Section (Bramham was divided into sections in those days). Oxford Blue was third and, as I had given up the office

job a year previously by that stage, it was really the turning point in my career, although I was under no illusions that everything was going to be easy.

In the autumn I applied to go to my first three-day event abroad, Achselschwang in Germany. We travelled out with Lorna Clarke and Liz Kershaw and we formed the British team which won, although no one quite knew how, as we went into the showjumping (which was in bottomless going) with four fences in hand, Lorna had five down and I had two! Liz, however, had a clear round on Just The Thing and finished seventh. Sir Wattie led the dressage despite everyone commenting on how ill and white I looked – so nothing's changed there! – and the cross-country, but our two fences down lost us the competition and we finished second to a Polish rider, Adam Prokulewicz. The whole trip was a marathon and the weather was awful, so when we got home to find I'd been accepted to ride Oxford Blue at Boekelo in Holland in a couple of weeks' time Jenny was absolutely horrified!

At the end of the year the selectors put us on the longlist for Los Angeles, but I just thought they were being nice and I didn't take it very seriously. I had really only competed in Scotland and the north of England and although I was quite well known up there,

'The press kept referring to me as "the new lad from Scotland", although when they discovered that I was thirty they quickly changed it to "Scottish veteran" ...'

above: Sir Wattie's owner-breeders, Dame Jean Maxwell-Scott and Susan Luczyc-Wyhowska

opposite: The start of our Badminton triumph in 1986

no one had a clue who I was when I turned up at Badminton the next year. The press kept referring to me as 'the new lad from Scotland', although when they discovered that I was thirty and married with two children they quickly changed it to 'Scottish veteran'!

Sir Wattie was my first cross-country ride around Badminton and, looking back, we were both pretty green. I made some serious mistakes but he kept bailing me out of trouble. He ended up having to climb over fences where I had got it all wrong and he was so genuine that he just kept going and, amazingly, gave me a clear round. My ride on him stood me in good stead for my later round on Oxford Blue at the end of the day and because I had a slightly better grasp of what was going on, it made him look the better horse, but I always felt that Wattie was really the best.

We were then shortlisted for the Olympics and asked to go to the final trial at Castle Ashby. It was obviously a great honour, but I have to say that the whole selection procedure as it was run then was a complete culture shock. Hugh Thomas, who is now Badminton director but who was a selector then, came up to me at the fund-raising Olympic ball and said, 'You might as well sell Sir Wattie as you'll never be on a team with him.' I was devastated and said, 'No, you've got it all wrong; he's a very good horse.' When Wattie won

Badminton in 1986 Hugh did have the grace to say, 'You were right', but at the time I thought it was the end of everything.

The squad then went to spend a week at Wylye with Lord and Lady Hugh Russell, which was a pretty scary experience in itself. Before we got there we received three pages of do's and don'ts, plus the times of meals. I managed not to commit any *faux pas* until David Green and I had a fight with a bar of soap which somehow ended up with a three-hundred-year-old dining-room window getting broken. In some trepidation I went up to the Russells' bedroom and knocked on the door. Lord Hugh came to the door and I confessed what had happened. In the background came the ringing tones of Lady Hugh: 'Somehow I feel sure that Mr Green had more to do with it than you!'

'David Green and I had a fight with a bar of soap which somehow ended up with a three-hundred-year-old window getting broken...'

Things went from bad to worse when Wattie tried to bank a parallel show-jump, came down in the middle and over-reached, so he was lame for a while too. It wasn't too serious, so when the final vet check came I decided to ride down to it to loosen him up; but I didn't realise that wasn't team training etiquette either, so there was more trouble.

However, it was announced that Lucinda Green, riding Regal Realm, Ginny Holgate (now Elliot) with Priceless, and myself with Oxford Blue were definitely to be on the team with the fourth place going either to Tiny Clapham with Windjammer or Robert Lemieux on The Gamesmaster. Sir Wattie would travel as a reserve horse. It was about this time that Richard Meade's great career, which included numerous valuable appearances on the British team, was coming to an end. He was fully expecting to be selected this time as well, and I found it absolutely incredible that after all he had done for the British team no one had the decency to warn him privately that he wasn't going to be selected. Instead he just had to sit there in shock as his name wasn't read out. It must have been quite devastating for him. I felt very sorry for Richard and it made me wonder what on earth I was getting into.

My horses came out best after the flight to Los Angeles, probably because they were already used to a lot of travelling down from Scotland. However, yet again I was rather taken aback to find that when it appeared that Windjammer might not be fit to run Tiny would take the ride on Wattie. No one had warned me that this might be the case – I thought he was *my* reserve horse, not the team's. Not only did we only have a short time to gain permission from the owners, but I was worried about how an eight-year-old would cope with a new rider at such short notice. In fact, Windjammer recovered and so it didn't happen. Nowadays the rules have changed and horses and riders have to qualify together for an Olympics, but in those days a good horse was considered the property of the whole team effort.

As Wattie didn't get his Olympic run on this occasion, I took him to Burghley instead that autumn, but it wasn't a great success. He tried to put a

stride in at a bounce of bullfinches and stopped. Next day I was horrified when he failed the trot-up and realised that he must have bashed his tendon sheath. He was then out of work for about eighteen months.

It was Jenny who did all the hard work in getting Wattie fit again. He absolutely adored her and would whinny when he saw her. Over the winter she hunted him and, when it snowed, she cantered him around a field in the snow. Of course, when I later tried to do a dressage competition in the same field, he thought he was there to canter about again, behaved appallingly and came last!

In the spring of 1986 Wattie came back into competition and gave me my first Badminton win. The event was, again, held in deep mud and as I was setting off on Phase A of the roads and tracks I was rather depressed to see loads of cars leaving. We were lying third after dressage, behind Bruce Davidson on J J Babu and Ginny Leng on Night Cap but Bruce had a stop in the Coffin and Ginny had a run-out in the Lake. The going was very sticky and no one got round inside the time, although Rachel Hunt did come very close. Wattie did feel tired towards the end of the cross-country, but he continued to jump beautifully and I couldn't have asked for more. We came home with 20.4 time penalties, which doesn't look great, but it was the fourth fastest. The weather was so bad that they brought the showjumping forward to the Sunday morning and wouldn't let any cars into the park. But people still parked in

above: Launching into space at Gatcombe 1986

opposite top: Relief at reaching the end of the cross-country at Badminton 1986 – a very wet year

opposite below: A proud moment for Wattie's groom, Claire Davies

'Wattie did feel tired towards the end of the cross-country, but he continued to jump beautifully …'

'Winning Badminton was the most fantastic thrill imaginable and afterwards we celebrated wildly with a motorbike race in the indoor school ...'

the village and surrounding lanes and walked for miles to come in and watch the showjumping. We had one fence down, but our good dressage mark of 46.8 had given us a decent advantage over Rachel and Piglet, and we won comfortably. The atmosphere was fantastic and Sir Wattie loved it – he always rose to the occasion in front of an audience.

Winning Badminton was the most fantastic thrill imaginable and afterwards we celebrated wildly with a motorbike race against Eddy Stibbe in the indoor school. Badminton's poor stud groom Brian Higham must have wondered what on earth had happened when he went to tidy up next day, but I think the tyre marks up and down the walls might have been a bit of a giveaway!

At that time Lucinda and Ginny were the most dominant riders at Badminton and when I wrote to thank the director, Frank Weldon, who was a great character and well known for his strong views on women competing, he wrote in reply: 'Glad to see a male winner – although don't get me wrong, I do like the women!'

In the autumn Wattie and I were selected for the 'alternative' world championships in Bialy Bor in Poland. (I had already been to the 'real' version in Australia with Oxford Blue, but this was a championships to make up for those who could not travel that far.) Bialy Bor was a good competition, but coming after a trip to Australia it was something of a marathon and Jenny was feeling fairly mutinous by the end of that year!

Our team was myself, Rachel Hunt on Piglet, Madeleine Gurdon (now Lady Lloyd Webber) on The Done Thing and Ginny on Night Cap. Ginny had just won the world championships in Gawler and was the reigning European champion and, in fact, went on to win in Bialy Bor too just for good measure. I suppose that she and I were the most successful British riders around that time but, probably because she's prettier than me, Ginny was definitely the favourite of our chef d'équipe, Lord Patrick Beresford. Over the years Patrick gave out some fairly classic instructions, but his aside before the cross-country at Bialy Bor really took the biscuit. 'Ian, when you go across country, try and ride a bit more like Ginny!' I didn't know whether to laugh or hit him, but fortunately I managed to see the funny side of it, and it still makes me laugh when I think of it now.

Wattie was a bit lame with a swollen fetlock on the morning of showjumping and so he had some treatment from our team vet's wife, Annie Scott-Dunn, who is a physiotherapist. This seemed to help, but then he stiffened up again and Peter Scott-Dunn didn't want to present him. But I thought it was worth a go, so I rode him around bareback, while dressed in my smart suit for the trot-up, and arranged for a chain of people to let me know when it was

opposite & below:
Wattie going at his very best through a combination at the Luhmühlen European Championships in 1987

'Glad to see a male winner – although don't get me wrong, I do like the women!' (Frank Weldon)

'So I rode him around bareback, while dressed in my smart suit for the trot-up ...'

above: Lap of honour in Luhmühlen with (left to right) Ginny Leng (now Elliot), Lucinda Green, and Rachel Hunt (now Robley)

opposite: On our way to team gold at Luhmühlen

about to be our turn. We managed to time it so that I cantered Wattie up to the trot-up, jumped off him and ran him up in front of the ground jury. They passed him when he had only completed two-thirds of the trot-up and, in fact, he was lame again straight away. Nowadays – and quite rightly – you could never get away with this sort of thing.

Anyway, we showjumped, the team finished first and we had two show-jumps down to finish third individually behind David O'Connor on Border Raider. Afterwards we found out that Wattie had a chipped bone on his fetlock joint, which healed naturally over the winter, which shows what a brave horse he was.

Badminton 1997 was cancelled due to the wet weather. Jenny and I were staying with the Vesteys at Stowell Park and Lady Vestey was designated to come and tell me the bad news, as no one else was brave enough! She says now that had she known me better at the time, she wouldn't have volunteered!

Our next success was the European Championships at Luhmühlen in Germany where the British team (Lucinda Green with Shannagh, Rachel Hunt on Aloaf, Ginny on Priceless and myself on Sir Wattie) won team gold by a substantial margin, despite Lucinda Green's fall from Shannagh. Rachel Hunt had a near miss on Aloaf, but somehow she stayed on and really saved the

'Although I probably make it hell for everyone else, I still think it's a good thing to feel nerves. You can't perform at your best unless the adrenalin is flowing.'

day. Ginny won the individual title, for the second time in succession, and I got the silver, both of us finishing on our dressage scores.

In 1988 I had the most fantastic Badminton and I suppose it is still the greatest moment of my career. Wattie was first favourite, at 5-2 with the bookies (you could bet on Badminton in those days) and Glenburnie was second favourite at 6-1. After dressage I was second on Sir Wattie and sixth on Glenburnie.

The course was enormous – it was Frank Weldon's last one – and there was lots of trouble. Riders like Ginny, Rachel, Lucinda and Mary Thomson all had falls and Angela Tucker, who was leading the dressage on General Bugle, didn't run. Only three of us finished inside the optimum time. So Glen went into the lead after his cross-country round and by the end of the day I was in a position to be first and second if all went well on Sir Wattie. It's always more reassuring for your second Badminton ride if the first one has gone well, but I still get very nervous. Although I probably make it hell for everyone else, I still think it's a good thing to feel nerves. You can't perform at your best unless the adrenalin is flowing. On this occasion the late Raymond Brooks-Ward came up to me with a BBC microphone to ask 'how I felt' as I was sitting feeling sick in the 10-minute box, which wasn't ideal, but I managed to give him a bit of nervous waffle and then it was time to set off. Sir Wattie gave me a fantastic ride and, sure enough, we went into the lead over Glenburnie.

There was so much razzmatazz next morning what with interviews and everything that somehow I forgot to walk the showjumping course, and by the time I remembered to do so the competition had started and it was too late. There was nothing I could do about it except watch some other riders and try not to panic. Dick Stillwell helped me by talking me

right: Exiting the Lake on our way to victory at Badminton 1988

*opposite: Launching
off the Normandy
Bank, Badminton
1988*
*below: Our lap of
honour*

pages 30–31:
*Warminp up at dawn
at the Seoul Olympics*

through it and relaying all the striding to me, but it obviously wasn't an ideal situation. Hugh Thomas was commentating and he remarked 'Typical Stark behaviour!' Glenburnie went clear though, and it was a peculiar feeling when I went into the arena on Sir Wattie because I knew I had already won; but I have to say that it was a very nice feeling! Amazingly, although Mark Todd and Blyth Tait have been first and second at Burghley, no one else has done it at Badminton and, so far, my record still stands.

Sir Wattie had a special year in 1988. He won all his spring one-day events, he won Badminton and he won the final trial. If it hadn't been Charisma, Mark Todd's wonderful little horse, who beat him at the Seoul Olympics, I would have been seriously put out because if ever a horse deserved an Olympic gold medal it was him. But Charisma was sixteen; he was a fabulous horse and he was the reigning champion after Los Angeles, so it was a fairytale win for Mark and much easier for me to swallow than if it had been anyone else who stole Wattie's thunder.

**'Hugh Thomas was commentating
and he remarked
"Typical Stark behaviour!"'**

Wattie had become much easier to handle by now, although he still often bucked the girls off on the way home from exercise, which he thought was very funny. He was not the best showjumper, but he tried very hard, and he became consistent in the dressage, considering he hated it so much. I would send Jenny out on him in a pair of rather obvious white draw reins because he had a very 'peacocky' way of going with his neck at a funny angle and if anyone else rode him it would take me ages to get him back on the bit.

The Los Angeles Olympics had passed in a blur because it was so overwhelming and frantic. Our children were tiny then, Jenny wasn't allowed to be with me, and the whole thing had been quite a strain. By contrast, Seoul was really enjoyable. We stayed in the Olympic village and went clubbing with the other athletes, particularly making friends with the swimmers and pentathletes. The best food seemed to be had at 5am, burgers and chips, which we liked because it was recognisable!

Rosemary Barlow had arranged for all the British supporters, including Sir Wattie's owners, David and Alix Stephenson of the Edinburgh Woollen Mill, to

'They would get "rent-a-crowd" in, which was generally masses of jabbering, shrieking small children ...'

stay in hotels around Seoul – the only trouble was that Rosemary didn't realise that they were also brothels! Each bedroom was standard, with very small beds, a loo, mirror, lamp and clock, and it was obvious to guests returning in the evening that their room had been used by someone else for another purpose during the day!

The Koreans had done a great job on the organisation at these Olympics and, because there was really no one there to watch, they would get 'rent-a-crowd' in, which was generally masses of jabbering, shrieking small children. Hugh Thomas had designed a good cross-country course which was demanding without being a nightmare and, although it was hot and humid, there were regular rainstorms which would clear the air. What I most remember is the flowers. There were no natural flowers in Seoul, but the Koreans had planted masses of pink and purple flowers along the track. But a few months later when I was doing a talk in Ireland with the late Irish rider David Foster about the Olympics, he was completely blank and couldn't remember them at all!

We had a few hiccups on the team. Mark Phillips, who was first to go, had to withdraw his horse Cartier in the 10-minute box due to pulled muscles and Karen Straker had a fall in the water with Get Smart, which has been forever immortalised by Lucinda Green's BBC commentary 'Sit up, sit up ... oh sh... sugar!' Ginny and I, however, had good rounds despite the heat, and we won the individual bronze and silver medals, while our overall team score was good enough for silver behind the Germans.

We retired Wattie after that as it had been such a fantastic year and we felt that it was a good note to finish on. Jenny hunted him that winter and one day, when I was on a young horse who was tired and needed to be taken home, we

right: On our way to team and individual silver medals. Ian and Wattie dwarfed by one of the incredible constructions on the cross-country course at Seoul

THE VICTORY CEREMONY

swapped. The moment I got on his back he went demented, lathered up and bucked his away across the field. The next time I hunted him he was equally daft and ended up somersaulting over on some ice.

After that I decided to give Wattie to the national hunt trainer Henrietta Knight, who was our chairman of selectors for the Seoul Olympics and who had always liked him. She wanted him as a trainer's hack and schoolmaster to run upside her young chasers. Hen rode him about herself and I warned her about his pathological hatred of tractors – he could hear them coming a mile off and would go beserk – but one day he spotted a farm implement hanging over a wall, whipped round and dumped her, breaking her wrist in the process! But he still was a wonderful schoolmaster and sometimes he would jump a hundred fences in a day. The jockeys laughed at him because he looked an unlikely racehorse, but he never missed his stride and was great for teaching the young horses to jump.

Wattie is still with Hen, living in luxury with his own yard. She absolutely adores him and every year he parades at open day as her yard mascot.

above: The mounted parade at the medal ceremony in Seoul
opposite: 'What I most remember is the flowers ...'
below: A little bemused as Ginny employs her own brand of entente cordiale

the perfect gent
Oxford Blue

Oxford Blue – known at home as Robbie – was a wonderfully successful event horse, considering that he really wasn't a natural jumper. If you didn't jump him every day he would literally forget what he was doing and you'd have to take him back to basics with a tiny crosspole.

The first time I saw him was with Polly Lochore, who bought him as a three-year-old and who first produced him, doing the working hunter class at the Royal Highland Show. I'm sure Polly will forgive me if I say that it wasn't a totally impressive sight! But I liked the look of the horse: he was a tall, weedy Thoroughbred, and looked as though he would be fast. I took him for a practice jump in the warm-up ring, which we ended up sharing with a lot of kids. They had the fences up quite high and weren't at all impressed with this group of adults who kept putting them down to the ground!

Polly had advertised Oxford Blue for sale and a friend of mine, Liz Davidson, who bred him with Nora McHattie, asked me if I would be interested in riding him for her if she bought him back. Although he wasn't the bravest horse, he had a good temperament, wasn't at all spooky and was very good in traffic, all of which made quite a pleasant contrast with Sir Wattie!

Robbie finished third to Sir Wattie at his first three-day event, Bramham, in 1983, and then I took him to Boekelo in the autumn. We finished seventh with a clear showjumping round, which was something of a rarity for him, and suddenly he was the one horse everyone wanted to buy. Richard Meade had been very keen on him, so was Clare Mason, although Lars Sederholm advised her that his jumping wasn't good enough, and Lorna Clarke also had someone who was interested. Jenny arrived in Boekelo to find me in a complete panic as serious money was being offered for Robbie and I was afraid I'd lose him. We rang Liz and explained the situation, but she was incredibly kind and said that she had no intention of selling. This was particularly generous in view of the fact that she was

'But I liked the look of the horse: he was a tall weedy Thoroughbred ...'

above: The gold medal team at Gawler in 1986: (from left) Ginny Leng and Priceless; me and Robbie; Lorna Clarke and Myross; Clissy Strachan (now Bleekman) and Delphy Dazzle
left: En route for third place at Badminton in 1984

one of those owners who doesn't really get any pleasure out of watching her horses at the actual events. She hated the crowds at Badminton and didn't like the attention. I think Liz only watched Robbie at one event, but she did love having him at home for his holidays.

We finished third at Badminton in 1984 behind Lucinda Green on Beagle Bay and Mark Todd on Charisma, having jumped a clear showjumping round, which I think ws possibly the last one Robbie ever did! Both my horses had finished inside the optimum time, which I think is probably what sealed my early reputation as a wild speed merchant with the powers that be! However, it earned us selection for the Olympics and, as I have recorded in Sir Wattie's chapter, a somewhat fraught period of team concentration before setting off for Los Angeles.

When I arrived at Wylye for team concentration, Robbie was lame with a pulled shoulder muscle, so he had some treatment from Annie Scott-Dunn. I had a dressage lesson on him but said that I didn't think he was up to too much work. However, to my disbelief, a dressage trainer who shall remain nameless asked me if he could ride the horse. Within half an hour the horse was handed back in a completely lathered state with the trainer announcing, 'He's good in his mind.' I was completely confused by all of this and felt rather

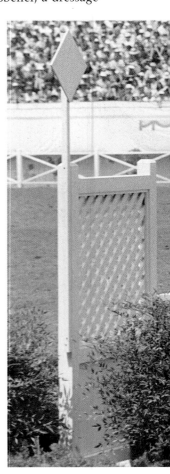

top: A wild time in the pool at Los Angeles and (above) in more sombre mood with Tiny Clapham

apprehensive, but a few days later I was really horrified to discover that circles of hair had come off Robbie's back. He was very sore and as a result I ended up riding him bareback for the next few weeks. He also had sarcoid scars which the man from the Ministry of Agriculture didn't much like the look of, so by this stage my blood pressure was sky high!

In Los Angeles we were third to go for the team and Robbie produced quite a good dressage test, which put us in equal seventh with Ginny. The whole competition was exhausting, as we had to drive a hundred miles to San Diego for the cross-country – there was a day off before and after cross-country, although the final horse inspection was still held early in the morning the next day – and the whole thing seemed to go on for ever.

above: *Silver medal celebrations (from left) chef d'équipe Malcolm Wallace, me, Ginny, Lucinda and Tiny*

left: *Robbie and I making our team debut*

below: *Celebrating victory with a water fight!*

I was so exhausted that I fell asleep on cross-country day and Wol (Malcolm Wallace, our chef d'équipe), was looking everywhere for me. It is, of course, a great honour to ride in a team for your country but one of the pitfalls is that team instructions can be quite annoying! As I was about to get on the horse to go across country, Wol said, 'Everyone's worried that you're going to go flat out and knacker your horse, so we'd really rather you went steadily and got a few time penalties. Then if you're going well at three-quarters of the way round you can go for it.' This wasn't the most helpful advice as Robbie was not a natural cross-country horse and he relied on having a bit of pace to jump fluently. He was, therefore, completely confused by being held back and consequently made a real mess of the second fence, which was a water trough. He hit it hard and ended up on his knees, I banged my nose, nearly fell off and dropped my whip. I was in a real panic, as finding yourself on an Olympic course without a whip is not

previous page:
A hairy moment on the cross-country in Los Angeles as we jump through what looks like a backlot from a Hollywood western

'Wol said, "Everyone's worried that you're going to go flat out and knacker your horse, so we'd really rather you went steadily and got a few time penalties …" This wasn't the most helpful advice …'

exactly ideal, but I heard a spectator say, 'Just take it easy', and somehow we got it all back together. When I got to the three-quarters mark, as instructed, I let Robbie go like the wind but it was too late and we came home with seven time penalties. It was fantastic to get a team silver medal at my first Olympics but I still felt a bit aggrieved that this strategy had perhaps cost us the team gold medal, as in the end we only finished three penalties behind the Americans, who won. However, Lucinda had what was generally considered a harsh dressage mark and Tiny had a fall in the water, so there were other factors to consider. I still felt, though, that Robbie never got enough credit on this occasion; he was only an eight-year-old and he was the only horse on the team who had been through Badminton that year, as the others were excused.

When we arrived back in London after the Olympics, Jenny was there to meet me at the airport, having flown down from Scotland with my mother, who had never been on a plane before. I couldn't understand why she was so anxious to whisk me away from the press conference, but she swept me back to Scotland and drove home from the airport at an uncharacteristically high speed – I am usually the fast driver in the family! – even going through a red light. I couldn't think what

left: *The 1985 European Champions parading at the Horse of the Year Show*

opposite: *An inauspicious appearance at Badminton in 1985*

above: *Robbie makes a celebrity appearance at the Edinburgh Woollen Mill after the Olympics; (right) a proud moment on the rostrum in Los Angeles*

on earth was going on, but as we arrived back in Ashkirk there were hundreds of people waiting and a party had been laid on in the village hall. The timing was brilliant, as twenty minutes later Les Smith, who had driven the horses home, arrived with them in the lorry. I couldn't believe the number of people who had turned up and was quite speechless. It was really more moving than the medal ceremony.

The next day I took Robbie to Carlisle for a TV interview. They wanted it to look as if we'd just arrived home triumphant from Los Angeles, so I had to lead him down the ramp, talk, and then lead him back up the ramp. Everything went well until it came to re-load him and he said, 'Oh no, I've done enough travelling,' and planted his feet. I wasn't very cool about media attention then and panicked slightly, saying rather audibly 'Come on you sod!'

After making such a dream debut at Badminton, of course my second attempt in 1985 was a disaster. Our house had been undergoing drastic building work and every window had polythene sheeting over it instead of glass. It was absolutely freezing and the whole family had flu. I felt ghastly, but as well as Robbie I had another ride called Lairdstown, who wasn't strictly qualified for Badminton, and I'd had to beg for special dispensation to run him. Frank Weldon had written to me and said, 'All right, you can run, but don't blow it!' so I felt I had to give it a go. We were eliminated four fences from home!

I then got on Robbie, who banked the wall into the

quarry at the start of the course and I promptly fell off. Mike Tucker was commentating and he said, 'Well, it was only last year that Ian Stark was third, but he doesn't look so confident now!' Lucinda Green was kind enough to point out that I had the flu, but I have to admit that it didn't look clever. All I wanted to do was crawl home and go to bed.

However, despite this unpromising display, the selectors still wanted Robbie for the Burghley Europeans that autumn. We won team gold and individual bronze behind Ginny on Priceless and were picked to go fourth in the team, which was quite something in only my second team appearance.

'... after we'd all been cooped up in a cottage for a month, tempers became quite frayed. I seem to recall a few arguments over how various things should be cooked!'

Next year we were on the team for the World Championships in Australia and we went into a month's quarantine at Wylye, along with the Irish and German teams. There were six of us on the world championship squad: myself, Ginny, Lorna, Clissy Strachan, Anne-Marie Evans and Mandy Orchard, and after we'd all been cooped up in a cottage for a month, tempers became quite frayed. I seem to recall a few arguments over how various things should be cooked!

However, despite the formality of Wylye, it was still a time of quite wild partying and after a few bleary appearances at the early morning trot-ups when I hadn't been to bed the night before, our chef d'équipe, Lord Patrick Beresford, took me aside for one of his inimitable little chats. 'Look Ian, I won't let the farrier get away with not shaving before breakfast and I don't expect to have to tell you either!'

One morning I certainly didn't dare tell him that I'd just come out of a police cell. During this time I also had five horses based in Mark Todd's yard at Cholderton. Toddy and I had been competing at Dynes Hall and had travelled in my car, but it was very wet and a lot of vehicles got stuck getting out so, to kill the time waiting, we decided to get stuck into drinking, especially as I'd won a class. I was far too pissed to drive, as of course was Toddy too, but in those days drink-driving was less of a political issue and he offered to drive. By the time we were on the motorway we'd had another drink at a pub and were stuck into some champagne when Toddy got stopped by police for speeding in the fog. Toddy was over twice the legal limit and I was incapable of driving my car, so we got clapped into Maidenhead cells for the night and, unfortunately, Toddy later lost his licence for a year!

He got his own back in Gawler, however, when we were waterskiing on the Murray River in the run up to the world championships. When it was my turn on the skis, Toddy, who was driving the boat, thought it would be very funny to speed up and do a very tight, fast turn, getting rid of me at high speed in the process.

As far as I was concerned, Gawler was another case of unhelpful team instructions. There was a double of parallels down a hill where I wanted to go the straight route. However, I was told to take the long route, Robbie slipped on the woodshavings and, after trying desperately to hang on around his neck,

'... so we got clapped into Maidenhead cells for the night and, unfortunately, Toddy later lost his licence for a year!'

below: Across country in the rolling hills of Gawler

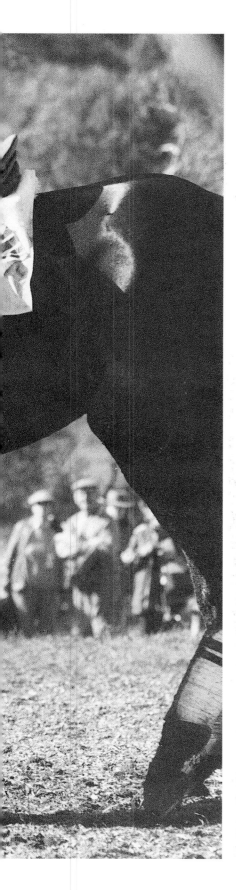

left: *Going, going ...!*
Desperately hanging
on around Robbie's
neck after our slip-up
at Gawler

I ended up falling off him within the penalty zone and clocking up 60 penalties. We still had the fastest time of the day though and, if we hadn't had that fall, when poor Tinks Pottinger was spun at the final inspection I would have had four fences in hand over Ginny to win the individual title. In fact, however, Robbie managed to have *four* fences down! Tinks's departure left the way open for Ginny to win the individual title and the British team the gold medal.

After Gawler we decided to retire Robbie. He was only only ten but he had a tendency to be stiff in the shoulder and at Gawler he had to be trotted up twice before he could be passed. Because he was so fast, I decided to do some hunter chases on him, but it wasn't successful. The first time we were tailed off on the run-in and the second time Robbie just managed one circuit and blew up. But he jumped very well on the racecourse – on our first race another jockey came along upsides and decided to try to half-length him (out pace him over the fences) but it didn't work as Robbie was too good at jumping at speed.

'If Robbie had been human, he would have been a city gent. He was very polite and house-trained ...'

We gave Robbie to Ceci Vestey, Hen Knight's sister, because she loved little Thoroughbreds like him, while Hen had always preferred Wattie. It was a great success; Ceci hunted Robbie and rode him in charity races. He was eventually put down at the age of eighteen after an accident in the field.

If Robbie had been human, he would have been a city gent. He was very polite and house-trained and behaved perfectly at publicity stunts. Once, when he was invited to open an Edinburgh Woollen Mill shop, he even walked around the counters!

the powerhouse
Glenburnie

Glenburnie's owner-breeder Bunny Maitland-Carew had high hopes of him being a racehorse – and I really do think that he would have made a Gold Cup horse – but, luckily for me, Bunny forgot to register him with Wetherby's as a foal!

'Glen was very wild and injury-prone ...The first time I rode him he barged sideways through the field ...'

opposite & below:
En route for second place at Badminton in 1988

Glen was the most powerful horse I have ever ridden, with the greatest stamina, and he could produce the most incredible acceleration at the end of a course. I think he would have been a wonderful ride as a racehorse, as he wouldn't have pulled and would have enjoyed galloping freely without having to be set up for combination fences. I once took him to racehorse trainer Nicky Henderson's Lambourn gallops where we easily clocked 40 miles per hour with scope for more when the end of the gallop came. Glen was very wild and injury-prone though and, in hindsight, I realise that we were probably getting him over-fit for the job as we were not used to preparing such a quality horse.

Bunny bred Glenburnie when he sent a racing mare he was given to the good racing sire Precipice Wood. Initially the idea was for Glen to be Bunny's wife Rozzie's hunter, but he was extremely naughty and, as a result, he was sent to me as a four-year-old to be disciplined. He certainly needed it – the first time I hunted him he barged sideways through the field – but he also gave me a great ride across country and jumped a metal gate, so I knew then that he was special. I schooled Glen a bit, which I really enjoyed, and eventually, thanks to the intervention of a wonderful dressage trainer called Eildon Watherston, it was suggested that I evented him. Glen won his first few events, which was a great encouragement to Bunny, and then the Edinburgh Woollen Mill stepped in and agreed to buy him for his eventing life.

Glen was impressive even as a six-year-old when he won the Scottish Novice Championships at Thirlestane Castle, although we had a near-miss when jumping into the road crossing. The road was his usual route back to the stables and

above: Our first Badminton together, in 1986

'I alternated between sitting in the saddle between fences and trying to kneel up on it ...'

opposite: Jumping into the Lake in 1989. Shortly after this Glen tripped and stopped, dropping us to 14th place

so he grabbed the bit and tried to turn right and I had to yank hard at him to keep him straight.

Glen's first three-day event was Chatsworth, where we were in with a chance of winning, but he tripped out of the water at Queen Mary's Bower and stopped. He still got placed though, and as my other ride Charlie Brown was higher up the line-up and another rider – Lizzie Purbrick – needed a horse for the parade, I lent him to her. Glen always managed to get attached to his stablemates – he later became inseparable from Murphy Himself and would scream the place down when he was out – and on this occasion he was desperate to be nearer Charlie Brown. He gave Lizzie an awful time and she said afterwards, 'I thought at first he was a nappy bastard but when I galloped him round the ring I saw why you like him!'

In 1986 I took him to Badminton as an eight-year-old, but withdrew him after the dressage, and rerouted him to Le Touquet in France. As I was about to go cross-country I noticed that the state of my stirrup leathers wasn't particularly healthy, but I carried on anyway. We got to fence seven, a drop fence with a left-hand turn afterwards and, sure enough, the leather snapped. I felt that I couldn't come all the way to France to go home at fence seven so I decided to keep going, but it was absolute agony. I alternated between sitting in the saddle between fences and trying to kneel up on it. Near the end of the course I suddenly realised that I was twenty seconds down on the clock so I galloped flat out at the last four fences to finish just one second over! Next day we showjumped clear, finishing fourth and winning the team competition, along with the individual winner, Ginny on Murphy, Richard Walker (Accumulator) and Clissy Strachan (Master Control).

In the autumn we went to Burghley. Edinburgh Woollen Mill had taken a hospitality tent and before my dressage I went and had rather a good lunch with their guests. I told the assembled company what time my dressage test was and no one noticed that I had the time wrong. I then went off to get on Glenburnie, ambled up to the dressage arenas and was rather surprised when everyone started shouting at me to hurry up. 'For goodness sake, I've got ten minutes,' I told everyone, to which someone replied, 'No you haven't, they're ringing the bell for you now!' Lucinda Green ran forward and pulled off Glen's tail bandage, someone else whipped off the leg bandages and I literally cantered straight from the collecting ring down the centre line of the arena. Unsurprisingly, it wasn't a very good first halt! The president of the ground jury, General de la Graviere, wanted to eliminate me because I was actually three-and-a-half minutes late, but fortunately Jook Hall persuaded him not to.

We eventually finished fourth after a very good cross-country round, but we were interviewed by Hugh Thomas for the BBC afterwards and we noticed in the recording that Glen was snuffling loudly into the camera. He had a tendency to make a bit of noise in his wind so we thought it would be best to send him down to the well-known horse vet Jeffrey Brain to be hobdayed, although I was rather put off when Jeffrey greeted me with the words, 'Ah, now you want his throat cut!'

The operation certainly helped Glen's wind, although it was after that he started his exhausting habit of snatching at the reins. He didn't pull when galloping in between fences, it was just when you took hold of him before a fence, and I never knew whether something was restricting him and making him uncomfortable.

Glen had quite a bit of time off after this. He was often injured because he was always bashing into himself and, if nothing else, we learned a lot about dealing

above: I won a £10
bet with Mark Phillips
for jumping the direct
route through the
S-fence at the
Burghley Europeans
in 1989

with horses' injuries while we had him. He had an awful habit of going sideways very fast and knocking his legs together. When standing quietly at the covert side out hunting with the rest of the field his favourite trick was to suddenly charge sideways through everybody, knocking them over, and then, just as everyone was picking themselves up, barge back the other way! In fact he could be a complete lunatic all round; one day the vet arrived just as Glen was being completely potty, having reversed into a fence where he was busily digging up the field, so I asked the vet how you could tell if a horse had a brain tumour. He said, 'Well I could shoot him and we could have a look, but that might be a bit drastic!'

I took him to Badminton in 1988 where he was absolutely brilliant and finished second to Sir Wattie. It was hard on Glen that he had to be second to another of my horses because he really deserved a Badminton win of his own. In fact, it was a sad truth that whenever I had two horses running at a major event, Glenburnie always finished just behind the other one.

I took Glen to Badminton in 1989 with Murphy Himself and the pair finished 14th and 15th, Glen having tripped out of the Lake and stopped. We were selected for the British team at the European Championships, which were again at Burghley, but that summer I had a crashing fall from another horse at Charterhall – which the Stark family has now renamed '*Charterhell*'! – and thought I'd broken my neck. Eventually I went to the renowned orthopaedic surgeon John Webb at Nottingham, who thought I had probably had a fracture which had then healed.

By the time Burghley came around I hadn't ridden for seven weeks and was on a strong diet of morphine. The team doctor pronounced me 'illegal' so I came off the morphine, which felt like how I imagine 'cold turkey' to be. I felt terrible

overleaf: The crowds gather at the start of the roads and tracks at Badminton 1990

and really shouldn't have been riding. Jenny and I were staying with Mandy Stibbe's parents, Mr and Mrs Jeakins, and I just couldn't sleep and ended up pacing the house every night. I think they thought I was mad and, funnily enough, we haven't been invited back!

As I went into the dressage arena at Burghley, a camera flash went off and Glenburnie reared and whipped around. It was probably the turning point in our relationship. From that moment on he definitely had the upper hand and, as Jenny says, he became pretty foul! At Burghley he ran away with me in the dressage, he ran away with me across country and in the showjumping. and he even towed me off my feet at the horse inspection!

Mark Phillips had designed the cross-country course and had built an S-shaped fence in the main arena with a very tight angle to the second element on

the direct route. No one had taken this route all day and, as I was last to go, I was quite keen to do it. As the rest of the team, Ginny, Lorna and Rodney, had all gone well, Jane Holderness-Roddam, our chairman of selectors, came up to me in the 10-minute box and said that if I wanted to do the direct line, it was fine. Then Mark Phillips came up and bet me a tenner I wouldn't do it, so that was it! By the time I got to the S-fence I was down on time anyway and I hadn't the strength to pull Glen around the slow route, so I just rode straight at it. It was a very tight turn but I hung on to his head and he did it beautifully. The crowd loved it and I've still got that £10 note signed by Mark Phillips! However, poor Jane got terrible stick for encouraging me to be 'irresponsible', especially in the light of the fact that Rodney's horse, Pomeroy, turned out to be unsound, which reduced us to a team of three for the showjumping. We still won the gold medal – and all three individual ones too. It was Ginny's third successive European Championship, which is a record; Jane Thelwall (now married to Malcolm Wallace) got the silver on King's Jester; and Lorna the bronze on Fearliath Mor.

above & opposite: **We were the first to go at Badminton in 1990**

'Then Mark Phillips came up and bet me a tenner I wouldn't do it, so that was it!'

In 1990 Murphy and Glen were fourth and fifth at Badminton, but Glen was very naughty in the dressage. Yet again he managed to knock into himself and had to be withdrawn. He was off for the rest of the year – he was a difficult horse to get two three-day runs out of in one year.

In 1991 Glen was sixth at Badminton behind Murphy, who was second, but

Murphy cut his stifle in the trailer after a subsequent team gallop so it was Glen who got to go to the European Championships at Punchestown; at last he was to get his own moment of glory. I really felt that this title would be ours and was determined that nothing would be go wrong. I did as I was told in eating pasta every night for energy, when in fact I was desperate for a steak, and I became so focussed that I forgot to collect Jenny and the children from the airport! However, my intense concentration didn't stop me going waterskiing with the whole team the day before the competition started, which earned me a very hard time from Patrick Beresford!

I lunged and schooled Glen in the area beside the dressage arena so that he would get used to it and, in fact, we were lucky enough to perform our actual test in front of virtually empty stands because, although I was fourth to go for the team, the dressage phase wound up on the Saturday morning. It was so quiet that I think Glen thought he was schooling! He earned his best ever mark – his first one in the forties – and I was quite confident, for the cross-country course, which was brilliantly designed by Tommy Brennan, had his handwriting all over it. Many of those designs are main features on Punchestown's course today. There were very few let-up fences and it caused quite a bit of trouble; Mary Thomson,

opposite: I'm not sure who's more out of control – me or Karen, who won the individual bronze medal with Get Smart

below: On the brilliantly designed cross-country course, at Punchestown 1991

for whom it was a first British team appearance, was in the lead after dressage but she had a fall at the penultimate fence, and Karen Dixon had had a run-out on Get Smart, but Richard Walker had gone clear on Jacana for the team.

Glenburnie was absolutely fantastic; winning the European title really was his finest hour. He pulled my arms out plunging in front of the fences, but there was never any doubt that he was going to go clear and fast. I think we were the only ones to take the direct route at the Newgrange Mound where you had to jump off the mound and over a big spread. Jenny says that seeing him come up that final hill is one of her greatest memories. He had such acceleration at full stretch that his withers would sink several inches nearer the ground as he galloped. It was wonderful and somehow meant to be that he showjumped clear the next day and the gold medal, my first individual title, was ours. The Irish welcome had been great all the way through these championships and they were very generous in the reception they gave me afterwards.

Needless to say, there were considerable celebrations when Britain won the team gold plus all three individual medals and, after a particularly good dinner, we set off in our sponsored Land Rover

Discovery to find the Irish party. The driver, an Australian spectator who had somehow got roped in, was sober, but no one else in the car was. Somehow we skidded violently on the wet road and crashed straight through someone's garden wall. The best thing seemed to be to hide the Discovery and hitch a lift to the party, but unfortunately we had left the number plate in the garden!

Next day I explained to Patrick Beresford that there had been a 'spot of trouble' with the car, to which he replied, 'Never mind old boy, it was a bit foggy.' He and Lorna Clarke went off to apologise to the garden owners, who hadn't realised what had happened until morning, and retrieved the number plate. I ended up re-painting the number on to the bonnet with Tippex and driving back to England in a limping Discovery!

Glen only went to one more major event and, sadly, that ended disastrously. It was Badminton 1992, which was very wet with slippery going and turned into a catastrophic competition where three horses died as a result of falls. Three fences from home was the Ha-Ha, a wide zigzagging ditch where most people had jumped slowly down into the ditch and up the other side. Only one horse had jumped straight across, but it was a fence that was well within Glen's scope and I felt that he would prefer to power straight over it rather than fiddle about with jumping in and out. But as he took off, his hindlegs skidded and he dropped vertically, back end first, into the ditch.

above: **The winning team at the Punchestown Europeans in 1991: (from left) Katie Meacham, Richard Walker, Lord Patrick Beresford, Karen Dixon, Lucinda Hanbury, me and Mary Thomson**

He landed backwards on my crotch, which was, needless to say, absolutely agonising. As I was staggering about, bent double, Lucinda Green said on the BBC commentary: 'I think Ian's hurt his wrist!' In fact, the injury was rather lower down! Anyway, Glen scrambled out all right and, rather than hang about, I hopped on him and galloped home as there were only two fences left. When I got back to the first-aid tent, a female St John's Ambulance lady asked if she could have a look at my injury, but I didn't think it was quite appropriate! Next day Glen was fit to showjump, but I certainly wasn't!

I was extremely upset, therefore, to receive a letter of reprimand from the FEI shortly after Badminton saying that my getting back on the horse after the fall was 'unsportsmanlike'. It seemed an unfair comment, considering that Glen had been perfectly all right to jump two more fences after the fall, whereas a lot of other horses had finished the course in a pretty bad state in the weather conditions but their riders hadn't been reprimanded.

'I was extremely upset, therefore, to receive a letter of reprimand from the FEI shortly after Badminton ...'

When we got home after Badminton Glen did show some bruising from his fall and he also had a haematoma. He was my reserve horse for the Barcelona Olympics, but he was rather anaemic that summer and we were worried about how he would fare in the heat of Spain. We took the decision to retire him and I paraded both he and Murphy at Burghley that September. The stewards instructed me to do just one lap of the main arena, but of course I couldn't stop and ended up doing two! Then I was asked to ride into the middle of the arena, remove their saddles, and lead them out. It was very emotional and everyone, myself included, was in tears.

Glen went hunting, where he was very naughty, and did a term as a school horse at the Warwickshire College, but I didn't want him to end up doing that for the rest of his life, so we lent him to Trevor Adams, the

master and huntsman of the Duke of Buccleuch's. Trevor is a great horseman who knows how to leave his horses alone while he is watching hounds, so Glen was actually a huge success as a huntsman's horse.

He eventually went back to the Carews at Thirlestane, where he was put down after having a stroke at the age of nineteen. His heart is buried at Thirlestane, right underneath the dressage arenas in fact. And for some mysterious reason, at the horse trials at Thirlestane the following year, a lot of horses were shying in the dressage arena. My horse was messing around too and I thought: 'I know you hated dressage Glen, but there's no need to come back and bugger up my test now!'

the one and only
Murphy Himself

As everyone knows, I famously gained the ride on Murphy Himself after Ginny Leng (now Elliot) swapped him for my horse Griffin. Murphy was the first horse that Ginny had bought on her own, without the advice of her mother Heather Holgate or long-time trainer Dot Willis, and she was very proud of him.

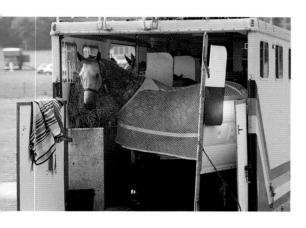

above: Murphy at Holker Hall in 1988

'"Well, I wouldn't have bought Murphy as a four-year-old; he's a great big ugly brute!" Ginny was not amused!'

He looked nothing standing still, and when you were sitting still on him he only felt about 15.2hh as he had a dip back, but when he moved he was the most impressive specimen and breathtaking to watch. Murphy was bred in Ireland and Ginny found him as a four-year-old – or at least she thought that was the case; in fact he was only three. I thought he was an awful looking horse. We were at a British team training open day once, talking to an audience about buying young horses, and my contribution was, 'Well I wouldn't have bought Murphy as a four-year-old; he's a great big ugly brute!' Ginny was not amused!

She took him to his first three-day event at Avanches, France, thinking he was a six-year-old, when in fact he was only five, and so he went to Le Touquet and Burghley, both of which he won, when he was only seven and not eight, as he was thought to be. But despite these successes, he was a desperately strong horse for a lightweight rider, even one of Ginny's undoubted talents, and my first real memory of Murphy is of him jumping her off at a double bounce at Chatsworth and then galloping back down the hill to the stables, jumping the string all the way. When she won Burghley on him, she had thrown away her whip at the first fence and wrapped the reins around her hand. Ginny had also started to lose control of him at one-day events and, as we all watched nervously on the closed-circuit TV at Badminton in 1988, he went airborne off the Ski Jump and catapaulted her into space, where she ended up breaking her ankle.

Ginny and I had started talking, although very much in a joking way, about swapping horses the previous year, although then it was Master Craftsman whom Ginny felt was too big for her. By the spring of 1988, however, Heather and Dot were hating watching her ride Murphy and had started to say that they couldn't support her competing him any more as they felt it was too dangerous. Talks continued and, as Ginny had a broken ankle, I rode a horse called Ballyhack for her at the Breda three-day event in Holland. I travelled out there with the Leng entourage – Ginny, Heather, Dot, and Val Gates of the sponsor, Citibank. It was certainly an education for me to do things their way – they made me ride in for so long before the dressage that my legs were shaking when I came out of the arena. Then Heather found a short cut on the roads and tracks which involved jumping a barrier on to the side of a motorway (Breda is an event situated underneath a motorway spaghetti junction!). I wasn't particularly keen on this idea, but I hadn't really got any choice as I was riding her horse. Anyway, to my relief, all went well and we ended up in fourth place.

'Heather and Dot were hating watching Ginny ride Murphy ... as they felt it was too dangerous.'

Shortly afterwards I had to come to London for a committee meeting of the Horse Trials Group events sub-committee, of which I was a member, so I took the train down to Heather's home at Ivyleaze in Gloucestershire and had a ride on Murphy. Ginny had warned me that he was a different horse at home and how right she was. I needed spurs and a dressage whip and he still felt like a riding

below: Despite being unseated on the cross-country, there was success at Boekelo in 1988

school donkey. I felt that perhaps this whole thing wasn't such a good idea.

Ginny pointed out that Murphy was a much better ride in a competition situation and so we agreed to have a 'secret meeting' at Weston Park, kindly arranged by the organiser there, Janet Plant. Griffin was a pretty little horse who I felt would suit Ginny, and after an initial hiccup when he stopped going into the water, they got on well. Meanwhile I decided to just drop Murphy into some fences to see how he would perform, instead of setting him up meticulously in Ginny style, a sight which gave Dot hysterics. Anyway, the upshot was that we went home with each other's horses.

Jenny was very upset when I returned home with Murphy. 'He's so ugly,' she kept saying. I then had to go away and do a week's teaching, so Murphy had a rest. Meanwhile Ginny rang up to say that she was happy with the swap, which threw me into a panic as I hadn't ridden Murphy once. However, we agreed to go ahead. No money changed hands but we had very formal contracts drawn up.

Shortly afterwards we both went to Boekelo. I had been riding Murphy in Ginny's citation bit, but I didn't think he needed it so I swapped it for a Dr Bristol. However, he was very strong at Boekelo, so back came the citation. On the cross-country Murphy took charge, skidded on a corner and pinged me off right over the string. However, it wasn't in a penalty zone and so we weren't penalised. He came home with his face covered in mud and, yet again, I had a visit from the FEI officials who didn't think it looked good. Apart from that it turned out to be a very happy outing as I won on Murphy and Ginny was third on Griffin. Dot said, 'You wait until next year; then Ginny will beat you!'

above & right: Sheer – and sometimes uncontrollable! – power: Murphy on the steeplechase at Badminton in 1989

opposite: *Into the Lake at the 1990 Badminton*

I had my one and only fall with Murphy at Belton the following year in an advanced class. We were approaching a complex with upright rails with a bounce to a sunken circle and another bounce to some rails. I knew Murphy would find the distance very short so I got hold of him and said 'whoa'. He struggled against my hand and, sure enough, we had a crashing fall. But I quickly learned that it was pointless interfering with Murphy before a fence because he could sort himself out. I had great faith in him.

I rode him at Badminton in a Dr Bristol, but he was such a handful that I also had to chuck my whip away at the first fence and, in fact, I never carried a whip on him again. He pulled so much, though, that we had a lot of time faults and we finished up in 14th place.

'I don't know who was the whitest in the face – myself or a horrified Heather Holgate!'

I still hadn't sorted out Murphy's bitting by the following spring of 1990 and I took him to Badminton in an American nathe bit which had worked well in the one-day events. However, when I got him on the steeplechase he was absolutely terrifying. I had no control and had to ride him with both hands on one rein. I don't know who was the whitest in the face – myself or a horrified Heather Holgate! There was no option then but to go back to the citation bit, but I didn't like riding him in it as it cut his mouth. Afterwards I hit on the idea of riding him in a cherry roller bit with combination noseband, which was the best I was going to get.

below: *Schooling at home*
pages 72–3: *Passing under the giant horse at Stockholm World Games*

We finished fourth at Badminton that year and were longlisted for the world championships at Stockholm, which was also the inaugural World Equestrian Games, a bringing together of all the equestrian disciplines. It was a fantastic competition; there was a brilliant atmosphere in Stockholm and team co-operation was very good. It was also a very pretty site – and unusual too. The route to and from the stables was shared with trams and the return on Murphy was always somewhat fraught. Eventually I just used to let him gallop home or he would fly-buck!

I was fourth to go across country for the team and by this time I was aware we were not in good shape: Ginny had had a fall with Griffin and Karen and Rodney had both had stops. Mark Phillips, who was then a selector, put the pressure on me to come home with a fast clear and he told me clearly to get a move on. He said, 'Don't forget that when you're galloping past trees you're not going as fast as you think you are.' As instructed, I took the long route at an early combination and then I went for it to make up the time. Murphy was incredible, bounding over fences and giving me the most powerful, brave ride. The course was not very suitable for him, because it was very stop and start

with twists and funny cambers, so he became fairly wound up. There was a sort of house fence which horses were meant to bank; it was huge and for one moment I thought Murphy was going to tackle it in one, but fortunately he did touch down on it. Everyone gasped when, at the road crossing combination, he bounced straight off the bank and over the next fence instead of taking a stride. Thankfully, I had anticipated this, or I would have been jumped off. By this stage he was totally in charge and I think he must have lost concentration because he hit the next fence, which was a straightforward parallel, very hard. This seemed to knock the stuffing out of him because as we got nearer home the lights went out and he came back a tired horse in the heat.

'I never quite got over the fact that he didn't win that year; it is one of my greatest regrets that he never won a major championship ...'

But Murphy was certainly the British hero of the day; his round had rescued the team, which then retained second place, although it was now behind the Kiwis instead of the Americans, who had been dressage leaders, and eventually we won the individual silver medal as well with a clear showjumping round. The only sour note was when we returned to England and Mark Phillips wrote a piece in *Horse & Hound* entitled, 'Ian's round is not to be emulated', saying that our round had set a bad example and was not the way to do it. He wrote, 'Ian's round was either going to end up with a medal or a very serious accident ... Missing out strides and standing off a long way is not good or safe riding and Scotty would not want any young or aspiring riders to emulate the way he tackled some of these fences.' I was absolutely furious and extremely hurt, not least because it was Mark's instructions that I should go for it. If we hadn't, we wouldn't have won the silver medal.

above: Ears back as usual! He was so strong in the showjumping we had one down, which cost us the victory

opposite: Murphy gives me the round of my life at Badminton in 1991

The next year at Badminton Murphy gave me the best ride I have ever had there. He was very impressive, totally in control of the situation without being crazy, and so powerful in the way he ate up the ground. I have never quite got over the fact that he didn't win that year; it is one of my greatest regrets that he never won a major championship of his own. There are so many 'if onlys' in this sport and, again, this was a combination of tiny factors – an error of course in the dressage test, a couple of cross-country time faults and then, when we were in the lead, he had, unusually for him, one showjump down. It was a triple bar, the easiest fence on the course, but he was pulling hard and just went through it. We just lost out to Rodney Powell with The Irishman, which was completely devastating.

As mentioned in Glenburnie's chapter, Murphy missed the 1991 Europeans because he had cut his stifle in the trailer. He bled inside the stitches and it was an

above: Murphy jumps into the water at Auchinleck with his usual ebulliance

'Barcelona was a complete nightmare and was probably the lowest point of my whole career'

awful mess. He was excused Badminton by the selectors the following year, 1992, with the Olympics in view, and then, after he won the final trial at Savernake, was chosen for the squad.

Barcelona was a complete nightmare and was probably the lowest point of my whole career. The three-day event was a logistical horror; we got lost every time on the way to the stables, it was very hot and the cross-country course was hours away.

Murphy did a good dressage test, although the heat rather got to him, and we were in second place individually with the team in the lead. It seemed that nothing could go wrong, but it turned into wholesale disaster and our team tactics and overall performance later received a considerable slating in the British press. Michael Clayton wrote in *Horse & Hound*: 'Britain blew it. There is no other way of explaining our worst Olympic performance for sixteen years.'

Richard Walker was first to go on Jacana and had a fall; Mary Thomson was

below: The cross-country at the Barcelona Olympics was difficult for all of us

'Suffice to say that the whole thing was totally unenjoyable, even more so when we were booed …'

next on King William, who became alarmed by the crowds and ran away with her so that she had to waste time doing all the slow routes; and Karen Dixon went very well on Get Smart, but was bitterly disappointed at the team instructions to take the long routes at the water complexes. I was fourth to go and Murphy had became affected by the heat. We went clear, but it wasn't enjoyable. He pulled hard on the twists and turns and then he hit the rails coming out of the first water quite hard, so he was a tiring horse by the final third of the course. Suffice to say that the whole thing was totally unenjoyable, even more so when we were booed as we took the long route at the last water complex. We ended up with over thirty time penalties, which was similar to Karen and Mary. However, the team was still in the lead and I was in fourth place individually.

Next morning Murphy came out rather stiffly, but he was sound and seemed to loosen up. By the time the final horse inspection came, he had stiffened up again and was definitely lame. I didn't want to present him at all and when, as I anticipated, we got sent to the holding box I begged the team officials not to make me re-present him, but because there was an Olympic gold medal at stake there was obviously pressure. So I ran him up for a second time, but I was feeling so miserable myself that of course it made Murphy miserable too and we must have made a pathetic sight. Of course the ground jury spun him, quite rightly. It was the end of the team's chances and a desperately sad note for such a wonderful horse to finish on. I was inconsolable and couldn't stand the thought of being cheerful and having to go to any more parties. I just wanted to go home and be with Jenny and the kids so I decided the best thing was to get out as fast as I could.

Murphy was retired after Barcelona and he embarked on a very successful new career doing lecture-demonstrations. Contrary to his public image, Murphy was a quiet and subdued character at home and, if you weren't careful, he would be bullied by other horses in the field. He was angelic with children and was perfectly behaved when tiny kids whose legs barely reached the bottom of the saddle flaps rode him. He wouldn't move until I told him to and then would trot very sedately around the school, taking great care not to dislodge them.

However, there was one very funny moment at a demonstration in aid of the Injured Jockeys Fund in Shropshire which I was doing with John Oaksey, the retired amateur jockey and racing journalist. There was a raffle, in which first prize was a ride on Murphy. John pulled his own ticket out of the hat and said that although he knew he should put it back, this was one prize he couldn't resist taking up. He got on Murphy and hitched his stirrups up, at which point Murphy realised that it wasn't a child on his back and took off. He flew around the indoor

opposite: A near miss when Murphy hits the rails out of the first water

below: Total dejection after Murphy is spun

'I was inconsolable and couldn't stand the thought of being cheerful ...'

'... in fact he was grinning from ear to ear – but I was completely grey with fright'

school at horrific speed. I don't think John realised just how out of control he was – in fact he was grinning from ear to ear – but I was completely grey with fright.

I hunted Murphy a couple of times and he would be all right until later in the day when the brakes would fail. Then, like Glenburnie, we lent him to the huntsman Trevor Adams and it was a huge success. Murphy adored the hounds – he thought they were his own – but he wasn't very well behaved at the meet where he tended to fly-buck and a lot of drink would get spilt.

Murphy's happy retirement was tragically cut short. A year to the week after Barcelona we received a phone call from Phoebe Stewart, who had all our horses when they were turned out, to say that Murphy had had an accident in the field and could we go up immediately. We arrived to find that, inexplicably, he had shattered his hock and would have to be put down. We still don't know how it happened. It was a terrible time because not only was it on the anniversary of the dreadful days of Barcelona but it also came just a few weeks after our groom Mark Holliday, who had looked after Murphy in Barcelona, was killed in a fall at Hexham horse trials. As Murphy will probably be the horse for whom I am most remembered, it was a sad ending.

right: The farewell parade at Burghley in 1992 with Glenburnie (right)

Jack the lad
Stanwick Ghost

After the success of the 'grey boys', Murphy and Glen, everyone said, 'You must have another grey.' And it wasn't long before I was being urged to go and look at Stanwick Ghost, who was bred by Sally Williamson at Scotch Corner. People kept on about how much I would love this horse so eventually I went down to have a look.

*top: Jack in winter wear and (above) almost
unrecognisable as the same horse as he shows
off at Badminton
opposite: At Hartpury in 1996
overleaf: Exercising at home at Beamsley with
Amanda Hartington*

I got on him and he went into this lovely medium trot, so I thought, 'OK, perhaps this is a good idea.' I then jumped him over some telegraph poles, which of course he couldn't knock down. Jenny remarked then that he had rather a dangling style, but we were sure we could cure him of that and, anyway, by this time I was in love with his charming attitude. He is a really sweet-looking horse.

Stanwick Ghost – 'Jack' – had a slight whistle in his wind, so I got some money knocked off the asking price, and then, as Sally had him already entered in a pre-novice at Hexham horse trials, I decided to compete him there and see what happened. Green wasn't the word for it. Although he looked pretty in the dressage, he stopped in the showjumping and then lurched around the cross-country, stopping at a triple bar. However, a month later I took him up to Burgie and won a novice class. But even then he was knocking showjumps down. He gives such a good feel that you don't realise his legs are dangling down over the jumps until you hear a crash underneath! He really couldn't care less about them.

The Edinburgh Woollen Mill had bought Jack initially, but when their sponsorship ended Lady Hartington decided to take him over. We had met over the years when we had been staying with the Vesteys at Stowell Park and Amanda Hartington had expressed an interest in owning an event horse. Now she is completely hooked! I took Jack down to the Hartingtons' home in Yorkshire for her to have a look at him and was met by an inspection committee which included

Stoker Hartington's racing manager John Warren. They were all impressed with Jack, despite his awful showjumping, and John said he wished some of his racehorses moved as well. In fact, Jack's parents had both been successful in racing and point-to-pointing and he had quite a good racing pedigree.

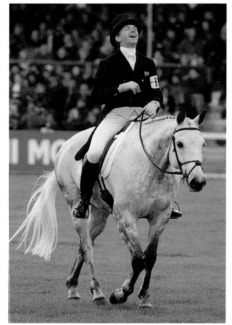

'I went in and galloped round, hooking and tugging, and somehow we had a clear round to finish second!'

I had a run of success on Jack. He won the Scottish Novice Championships at Thirlestane – with a clear showjumping round! – and was a gutsy fourth at Blair Castle three-day event in very wet weather. I then took him to Saumur in France in 1993 as a seven-year-old where it was a very big track. Mike Tucker, who was chef d'équipe to the British riders, kept suggesting that I took the long routes but, with rather more confidence than I was feeling, I said, 'No, I'm going to go straight' and, in fact, Jack was great and had a clear round. Next day he worked in really quite well over the showjumps but still looked rather dangly, leading Mike to comment, 'Rather you than me.' Anyway, I went in and galloped round, hooking and tugging, and somehow we had a clear round to finish second! Sadly, it was the one time that Amanda wasn't there to watch him.

I took him to Blenheim in the autumn where he went well across country but felt rather flat next day and I couldn't get him

above: Relief or disbelief? Ian's reaction to their leading dressage score, Badminton 1996
right: The support team (l to r) Sheila Dolton and Sharon Kitson (groom and head girl to Lady Hartington respectively), Lady Selina Carter (daughter), Lady Hartington, Ian, Lady Vestey, Lord Vestey, Jenny and Caro

to jump a single pole clear. Steve Hadley, a former international showjumper and commentator, was watching and I asked him what I should do. He said, 'Well, I think you've tried everything!' In fact we only had two fences down and finished fourth.

I took Jack to Badminton as an eight-year-old and all was going well until we had a fall coming out over a walled corner out of the Quarry. Jack didn't mean to stop, but he got too close to the fence, which was at the top of a steep slope, and

above: *The squad off to walk the course in Atlanta: (from left) Charlotte Bathe, chef d'équipe Charlie Lane, Karen Dixon, me, Leslie Law, Mary King, Gary Parsonage, William and Wiggy Fox-Pitt*

tipped over. He got cast against the fence, with me pinned underneath by the leg, but he wasn't at all concerned and started to graze happily, seemingly unconcerned by the fact that he was stuck. And after we disentangled ourselves, he carried on stuffing his face, by which time the crowd was roaring with laughter.

As Jack was none the worse for this tumble, I took him to Punchestown a fortnight later. He did a brilliant dressage and a fantastic cross-country, which showed that he had lost none of his confidence after his Badminton fall, but then he had four showjumps down and dropped from first to eighth place.

After that he had a long time off work, as at his first outing in the autumn of 1994, where he won the advanced class at Auchinleck, he struck into himself when tripping out of the water and damaged a tendon, necessitating eighteen months off.

Jack came back at Badminton in 1996 in brilliant form. He did a fantastic dressage and gave me a wonderful ride across country to put us in the lead, but we didn't have a showjump in hand over Mark Todd on Bertie Blunt. Jack seemed to be jumping well and I had started to dare to believe that we might win when suddenly he had the gate down, which was the penultimate fence, and then flopped feebly through the last fence. We dropped to sixth place, but while I was naturally disappointed, I felt that he had at least tried this time and that there was some hope.

We set off for the Atlanta Olympics with high hopes. The build-up was quite

'And after we disentangled ourselves, he carried on stuffing his face ...'

tense because the squad had to fly out to America so early for acclimatisation purposes and it seemed an awfully long time to be sitting around with just one horse to ride. Believe it or not, reading books and swimming can get boring after a while and you start thinking about all the things you could be getting on with if you were at home. It's a long time for a group of riders and officials to be cooped up together and, from time to time, things can get tense. Jack also gets bad-tempered as he is quite a big-bodied horse and has to be put on a diet for major competitions. It changes his character, as he is a cuddly person at home, but starvation makes him very cross! He starts biting people and before we set off for Atlanta he bit a chunk out of the chest of Bernie Tidmarsh, the Badminton farrier, and he also bit a couple of the grooms.

'Starvation makes him very cross! He starts biting people and before we set off for Atlanta he bit a chunk out of the Badminton farrier ...'

However, I did actually enjoy Atlanta very much – at least until things went wrong! Gone are the ridiculous days of team orders that riders can't be with their partners. It was also great to have Stephanie and Tim there too, and with the Hartingtons we all had a really fun time together.

The organisation at Atlanta, too, was superb. It was in the back of everyone's minds that this could be a repeat of the disastrous world championships of 1978 at Lexington in the States where the heat and humidity took such terrible toll on the horses, and I think we were all secretly worried as to whether our horses would be the same again. However, incredible care was taken in Atlanta; all the exhaustive experimentation and research paid off and the horses came out of it absolutely fine. It was, however, a bit disconcerting setting off on Phase A in virtual darkness! Cross-country day started at 6.45am and I was second to go after Blyth Tait, which was quite an effort as I have never been good in the morning!

I was in the lead after the dressage with Jack's best ever mark – 35.2 – and the team was second, just behind the Americans. However, unbelievably after Barcelona, this was destined to be another British humiliation at the Olympics.

Jack was going brilliantly across country when we had a horrible fall at fence 11, a brush fence out of water, where he tripped at a lip of ground coming out of the water. (Later this water was dyed violent blue for the individual competition so that horses could see where they were going.) Jack didn't seem to see what he was doing – he may have been transfixed by the brush fence in front of him – and afterwards we realised that his foot had probably got stuck, which caused him to trip. He sent me flying neatly over the fence and was himself suspended in the air over it, but fortunately he didn't follow me over or he could have landed on me. I had always secretly wondered whether Jack was a brave horse or just a good-looking poser, but the way he went across country after that fall made me realise that he really did have courage. He was great for the rest of the course, but it was a deflating start for the team and a situation from which we never seemed to recover.

William Fox-Pitt had a stop on Cosmopolitan at a bounce fence and then lost more time with a fall on the flat, Gary Parsonage had the best round of all of us on Magic Rogue, and Karen had a slow clear on Too Smart, by which time we were out of it as a team.

Next day Jack hit three showjumps, but we were too far behind to get into the medal position anyway . Thus ended another disastrous Olympics for Britain, which was followed by the predictable damning inquest in the press. Much of the criticism centred on the fact that people thought it was a case of 'too many cooks' – too many selectors, chefs, trainers and other interested parties trying to tell us all what to do, while those of us who had been trained by others outside the official team trainers were accused of making life difficult for Ginny Elliot, who was appointed jumps trainer.

top: Proof of our best-ever score

above: Jack takes the Olympic atmosphere in his stride and enjoys a nap

Before the Olympics I, along with Mary King with King William, had been to the world-renowned trainer Lars Sederholm for help with Jack's showjumping and, although it became irrelevant in the end in Atlanta, Lars had been a wonderful help to me. He is probably the best trainer in the world; some of the greatest riders have been taught by him, and he has a tremendous understanding of horses. He loose-schooled the horse and got us both to relax, which gave me confidence, and he also worked on our canter work, trying to get Jack into more of a showjumping shape than a dressage shape. But he explained to me that Jack had quite a difficult temperament as far as showjumps were concerned and a bit of a temper. He explained that the short bouncy canter required did not come naturally to Jack and said that he must not be forced into it, or he would screw sideways over the fences and the problem would get worse. Above all, Lars explained that I must just try and see the funny side of showjumping Jack and not try to ride him like other horses. Although Jack's showjumping problems at three-day events were probably incurable, Lars restored my confidence and made me realise that my riding of Jack had become a bit negative and defensive.

On returning from Atlanta, however, I yet again had cause to be annoyed with Mark Phillips. This time he wrote in *Horse & Hound* that not only was the cross-country fall my fault, as was the opinion of Sue Benson in *Eventing*, too, but that Lars's training methods had been a waste of time! I was pretty annoyed about the criticism levelled at me, but I felt it was unforgivable to be rude about a trainer of Lars's reputation. However, this is something I have learned with the press; there is very little redress and you just have to get on with it.

Although I had just about swallowed losing Badminton in 1996, the following year I was not so philosophical. Again we were in the lead after the cross-country, Jack having given me a brilliant, confident ride

above: At the Olympic trial at Hartpury

right: Bottoms up at Badminton in 1997!

opposite: Jack gave me a brilliant ride at Badminton

which really thrilled me. Next day, though, he was ominously flat in the parade of competitors – usually he shows off and goose-steps. He had no spring to his jump at all in the practice ring and was not giving me a good feeling.

Once in the arena, he managed to knock down the first three fences, which was incredibly depressing, followed by three more. The first and third fences were parallels and he caught them with his back legs, which he didn't usually do. We plummeted to 13th place and left the arena very dejected. Fortunately everyone seemed to know how devastated I was and left me alone. We went back to the stables where Jack went to the back of his box and looked miserable; he seemed to know that it had all gone wrong.

I trotted him up the next day for the selectors and Andy Bathe, our team vet, was happy with him. However, over the past year we had discovered melanomas

*Opposite: Jack read
the script at the
new Chatsworth
CIC in 1999*

in Jack's throat and Andy wanted him to go to Newmarket to be checked out again. As it happened, the melanomas weren't causing trouble, but while Jack was in Newmarket, it was noticed that he had heat in his front legs so we got him checked out to find that there were problems. Obviously the poor horse had been feeling sore, which was why he had been so out of sorts on the final day at Badminton. He had some new injection treatment from America and then was on a programme of controlled exercise for a year. I competed him twice at the end of 1998, finishing third at Parkgate and first in the advanced at Bishop Burton and it was great to have him back enjoying himself, but we decided that he should not do any more three-day events.

*above: Jack with his
fan club: (left) Lady
Hartington's
headgirl, Sharon
Kitson and (right)
Amanda Hartington*

We were placed in a couple of one-day events in the spring of 1999 but the aim was the CIC (international one-day event) at Chatsworth, which is the home of Amanda's parents-in-law, the Duke and Duchess of Devonshire. The last event at Chatsworth had been ten years before and it was Amanda's ambition to see another one run on this beautiful site which is so perfect for a horse trials. Amanda was closely involved with the organisation of the event, which was being run by a great couple called Mike and Sue Etherington-Smith, who I had introduced to Amanda at Blenheim previously. She rang me up one day and said, 'I've just seen the trophy; it's beautiful and you've got to win it!' There were more jokes along this vein and by the time Jack had paraded at the press preview, expectations were running ridiculously high.

It is very rare with horses that a plan to win a specific competition comes off; it is generally best not to place too much emphasis on one event, as so much can go wrong so easily. Therefore it really was amazing that Jack won Chatsworth. He hadn't even done a particularly good dressage test, which masses of people trooped down to watch, but he only had one fence down on what was a difficult showjumping track. The one thing I have now learned is not to overwork Jack before his dressage, as it takes the edge off his showjumping. A lot of riders had come to watch, probably expecting us to crash through loads of fences, and Jenny and Amanda had warned me that if I had a lot down they weren't coming near me!

'She rang me up one day and said, 'I've just seen the trophy; it's beautiful and you've got to win it!"'

I was lying equal third at that stage and when I heard that Leslie Law, who was below me, had gone very fast into the lead on Shear H_2O, I thought, 'Oh god, I'll have to go for it now.' Jack is fast across country, but I don't think I've ever been that fast on him. He just spun round the course, flying over the corners without hesitation, and was just so balanced and sure-footed. It was fabulous and will

opposite: Jack posing for the camera at the Chatsworth prize-giving

above: Jack makes a neat jump over a narrow fence at Bicton in 1999

overleaf: A fabulous backdrop for a photocall: me on The Moose, and Amanda on Jack, with Stoker Hartington at Chatsworth

always stick in my memory as one of my great rides. We went into the lead and stayed there, as Karen Dixon and Blyth Tait, who had better dressage marks than me, had had stops while Pippa wasn't quite fast enough and finished second.

It was wonderful for everyone that we won – a really happy result which made up for everything. I was asked to come to the prize-giving mounted on Jack, something you couldn't do with every horse as lots of people were crowding around the presentation area. Crowds of children clustered around him to pat him, feed him Polos and get autographs and he was so good; he just loved the attention.

'Crowds of children clustered around to feed him Polos and get autographs ...'

Jack's next outing was the new CIC at Thirlestane Castle in August. He was in the lead before cross-country, having jumped his first clear showjumping round for years, but as we were waiting at the start of cross-country there was a hold-up. We all knew that Polly Phillipps had had a fall from Coral Cove, but none of us realised at first how serious it was. About twenty minutes later we were told that the event was going to be abandoned but of course we couldn't be told why, as her husband Vere had not been contacted by that stage. But we all guessed the horrible truth, that Polly had been killed, and it was a very strange atmosphere because no one knew what to say or do. And because it was Polly, of all people, who had been the centre of such controversy all summer because of the Coral Cove doping case, it was somehow all the more terrible and dramatic, a tragic end to probably the most extraordinary saga ever in horse trials.

I managed to give Jack one last run in 1999, at Witton Castle where again he showjumped clear in the advanced. I had decided by this stage that the only technique to employ with him in this phase is that of riding like a demented twelve-year-old on a 12.2hh pony! We flew around, giving him no time to think and just winging around the corners – goodness knows what it looked like, probably not very pretty! However, he then did a wonderful cross-country round and we won.

The cross-country starter said to me, 'Please bring him back next year as we love seeing him,' but in all honesty I don't know how much more competing Jack will do. Amanda adores him; she has him when he is not competing and does all his fitness work, and above all I want him to have a happy retirement with her, doing some hunting. I don't want her to end up with an injured horse she can't enjoy, so I may not ride him much more, although we haven't ruled out the possibility of another Chatsworth. Jack started as a young horse and you can't compete a horse at top level at both ends of his career, but watch this space!

The Kiwis

Over the last few years I have got into buying New Zealand horses. The phenomenal success of the New Zealand riders like Mark Todd, Blyth Tait and Andrew Nicholson in the 1990s has shown that they really do have fabulous horses who tend not only to be classy thoroughbreds, but are tough and agile thanks to their healthy upbringing running loose on rich, grass-covered hillsides. I would not wish anyone to be under the impression that I think New Zealand horses are better than British horses – that isn't necessarily the case and it must remembered that we see the best of them in England – but they do tend to be more available. It is amazing how hard it is to find horses in England now, whereas in New Zealand, if you see a young horse you like, the chances are that it will be for sale, as that is how many Kiwi riders make their living and their reputations.

the original
Arakai

Arakai was bought at the Auckland bloodstock sales by Gee Davidson, who got him for a decent price as he'd fallen off the horsebox ramp and was well bandaged, which looked slightly suspicious. Gee is very good at producing horses – she was also responsible for Andrew Nicholson's 1998 World Games ride New York – and she won the one-star three-day event at Puhinui on Arakai.

top: Badminton 1997 was a big test which Arakai passed with flying colours

He caught the eye of Vaughn Jefferis, who was then the reigning world champion, and Vaughn eventually bought Arakai for the Taupo three-day event in New Zealand, where he finished tenth.

Vaughn renamed him – Arakai's original name was Be Happy – brought him over to England in 1996 and kept him with Lynne Bevan, who rode him in a few events. Out in Atlanta I talked to Vaughn about how I was looking for another horse and he suggested I had a look at Arakai. I went to see him, but at first sight I wasn't sure. Arakai has very high withers and not the best of hocks. He was also rather skinny and his flatwork wasn't great. However, I really liked his jump and I persuaded the Vesteys to buy him.

above & opposite: Jumping under the Lion Bridge at the Burghley Europeans 1997

previous page: Rangitoto at Blenheim in 1999

Our first three-day event came a couple of months later, at Boekelo in Holland, where he gave me a good cross-country ride apart from a run-out at a naturally Y-shaped treetrunk, a regular feature at Boekelo, where he didn't really understand the question and ducked out at the last minute.

When I took him to Badminton in 1997 he was only eight and had really had very little mileage. There was a bit of controversy that year as Badminton was so over-subscribed that the foreign riders were only allowed to ride one horse and I was one of four British riders who were allowed two. There was, therefore, a bit of bad feeling, not to mention a lot of press comment about the situation, but I just had to try and ignore it as I was keen to see how Arakai would run, and so were the selectors.

Jack was my second horse and so Arakai and I found ourselves drawn first of everyone to go. Arakai was a bit tense in his dressage due to the atmosphere, but he

gave me the most fantastic cross-country ride, apart from being a
little green at the Coffin. Arakai is by Ring The Bell, the same sire
as Blyth Tait's good horse Aspyring and also the 1997 Grand
National winner Lord Ghyllene, and really he galloped and
jumped with his ears pricked every bit as well as his racehorse
relation. We finished 14th, which was a great result for his first
four-star, but Ceci Vestey wasn't sure whether he was ready to be
put under the pressure of team selection for the Open Europeans at Burghley in
September that year.

However, I was always quietly hopeful that I might be able to change her
mind and, anyway, the selectors still invited me to run Arakai at the final team trial
at Thirlestane. He went so well that it became obvious that he should be allowed to
go to Burghley on the team.

We were picked second to go for the team and by this stage Arakai's dressage
was much better and had improved by some 20 marks from his Badminton
performance. The cross-country course had caused a fair amount of trouble, but he
gave me a brilliant cross-country ride, finishing clear and inside the time despite the
fact that my watch had stopped and I hadn't a clue what speed we were doing. Mary
King had done a great job pathfinding for the team on Star Appeal; Chris Bartle,
who was third to go, had an unlucky fall from Word Perfect, but then William Fox-
Pitt had the most brilliant round on Cosmopolitan to put us in the lead.

Things were a bit tense next morning when Cosmopolitan was sent to the holding box at the final horse inspection. I was inclined to advise William not to re-present him, remembering my horrible experience at Barcelona with Murphy, but both William and Andy Bathe were confident that Cosmo would pass and, at the end of what had been a somewhat controversial inspection overall, he passed.

In fact, while Mary and I had two showjumps down apiece – I blame myself a little for this as I probably let Arakai float around too much instead of really riding him – Cosmopolitan had a clear round and we won the team gold, beating the New Zealanders. It was a fantastic feeling winning on home ground and, for William, Mary and myself, it definitely helped to erase the unfortunate memories of Atlanta.

Sadly, next spring Arakai showed a little roughness in the leg. Andy Bathe wasn't too worried until the second scan, which showed a definite, although tiny, shadow on the tendon, so Arakai had the whole of 1998 off.

He came back in the spring of 1999 and we led the dressage at the new advanced event at Rolleston, although I withdrew him before cross-country as the going was so deep.

There were high expectations of Arakai at Badminton, but I was a bit disappointed with his dressage as he was still tense and I felt he should have got over this. Badminton does tend to have this effect on a lot of horses – I think somehow Burghley is easier because there the horses have already been in the dressage arena for the first horse inspection and aren't quite so overawed. Also, Burghley's arena has a wider entrance which isn't so near the grandstand seats.

After I'd ridden my first horse, Jaybee, across country I went to the press tent to be interviewed as I was in the lead at that stage, and I was even relaxed enough to have a lunch of chicken curry followed by a sleep. The weather was terrible with continuous torrential rain and Jenny was wondering whether I should run Arakai: every time we glanced at the closed-circuit TV there seemed to be carnage with someone else landing on the floor covered in mud. By the end of the day the scoreboard was a mass of lines, Rs and Es. There were twenty-seven falls and only thirty-one finishers, which by today's standards is not a great statistic.

right: **En route** *to team gold at the Burghley Europeans:*
Arakai clears the Waterloo Dragon

'I rolled around on the floor

clutching my stomach in agony.

Arakai meanwhile galloped off

in great glee ...'

When I got on Arakai at the start of Phase A he felt pretty wild and extremely well, so I felt I had to have a go. Everyone was reporting that the steeplechase was riding very heavily by this stage – even Mark Todd, who was leading after the dressage on Broadcast News, had had twenty-one time faults – but I thought Arakai would be all right. However, he gave me a fright at the first fence when he got stuck in the mud but somehow managed to get over and then at the second, where I saw what should have been a good stride, he pulled off a shoe and crashed into it. I was well and truly unseated and rolled around on the floor clutching my stomach in agony. Arakai meanwhile galloped off in great glee and I decided that it would be sensible to retire! But then there was problem of what to do with Arakai, as I certainly didn't to ride him back to the stables and no one wanted to lead him either. In the end he went back in the horse ambulance but he was so cross at not going across country that he kicked hell out of the trailer and broke the bar!

I think in hindsight that we probably got him too fit for Badminton; I hadn't wanted to give him too many runs because I was worried about his legs and also he loses weight easily. When we first had him he used to box-walk but now he is more settled. He is not a horse that you can just load up and travel; his whole schedule has to be carefully stage-managed.

Burghley in the autumn of 1999 provided his first three-day cross-country day for two years, but he hadn't forgotten a thing. It was one of the biggest courses I have ever seen and, in my opinion, almost over the top. I had thought the ground jury was rather chicken when they took out the second of two enormous picnic tables near the end of the course but, although I think Arakai would have jumped it easily, I now realise that their decision was the right one.

It was a hot day but Arakai went brilliantly, clearing every fence by miles to put us into sixth place and I was absolutely thrilled, but when I got off him in the 10-minute box, someone told me that another rider Simon Long, who had gone across country before me, had died in a fall. This was the fourth fatality in the year and had come only two weeks after Polly Phillipps, whose funeral it was the day before. I felt quite numb; it was unbelievable, and it did undoubtedly cast a sad shadow over the rest of the weekend.

Ironically, Arakai had only hit one fence, an upright mock-castle at the penultimate where he stood off too far and clipped it with his front toes, but he must have dropped his hindlegs on the fence because later that evening he started to stiffen up behind. Andy Bathe was looking after him and decided to give him an X-ray, in which we discovered that he had chipped a tiny piece of bone off the patella of his stifle. It was not only a terrible disappointment after he had gone so well, but was also a worry as it meant he would have to have an operation and there is always the uncertainty about what effect an anaesthetic will have.

But it turned out that the bone chip was nowhere near any of the ligaments and he came out of it very well and with his front legs in good shape, despite their previous injuries so, after a winter's rest, I have high hopes for his outings in 2000.

the flying kiwi
Jaybee

Jaybee was produced by Bryce Newman, a New Zealand rider who returned home some years ago where he is very successful on the national circuit and has made a great name for himself producing horses.

'He was horrified by the snow. Amanda found him trying to stick his head in a stone wall to get away from it ...'

above: The new arrival in January 1998, with Sharon

opposite: Clearing a corner at Bramham, in 1998, where we came 14th

I met up with Bryce at the Adelaide three-day event in 1997 and primed him that I would be looking for a horse when I arrived at the Puhinui three-day in New Zealand in December. Bryce told me that he had a nice little brown seven-year-old that I would like and when I saw Jaybee working in Bryce's school I took to him straight away.

Jaybee is small and lightweight and a good jumper. He is one of the very few horses that both Jenny and I have liked from the start, perhaps because he reminded us of Oxford Blue, except that Jaybee is a better jumper. I rang Amanda Hartington straight away to tell her about Jaybee and she was very trusting because she agreed to buy him unseen, unless you count looking at a video.

As Jaybee was only rising seven, I asked the organisers of Puhinui if I could ride him in the two-star class, but they said that he had too many points. This meant that I just had to get on with it and ride him in the three-star, which was a rather nerve-racking prospect, but I thought at least if all went well it would be a useful qualification. The problem was that as I'd virtually committed Amanda to buying him by this stage, I was terrified of laming him.

I took Jaybee cross-country schooling before Puhinui and Bryce advised me to put some big studs on him. Riding him into a water jump, we skidded to a stop and all but fell four times. I was wondering what on earth I was doing riding this donkey when it suddenly dawned on me that he didn't have the studs on!

I then took Jaybee to Puhinui where cross-country day got off to a rather shaky start. Phase A used some of the same route as Phase C so there were other horses going past us, which caused Jaybee to freak. He spooked and galloped off after another horse and was completely panicked, so I just made him stand still and look out to sea while he got his confidence back. This seemed to work and we achieved the steeplechase and Phase C without incident. When we started off

across country I had no idea what to expect, but he really did give me a brilliant ride and by the end I realised that I'd bought a good horse. I did opt for some of the slow routes, but I also took on some big corners and he went very well.

Next day Bryce advised me to sit quietly on him in the show-jumping. While we were practising I said, 'Can't I let him hit one?' and Bryce replied, 'No, that'll upset him!' So when we got into the ring we made a real mess of the first fence. If I'd had enough impulsion it would have been all right, but we ploughed through it, I lost a stirrup and Jaybee galloped off leaving me hanging round his neck with my backside in the air. And, naturally, this was the picture that ended up in *Eventing* magazine, which didn't please me at all! Jaybee jumped like a stag after that, except at a combination where he got unbalanced and hit another fence, but we still finished ninth and I was pretty impressed with him.

Jaybee got off to an unfortunate start to his new life in Britain as he suffered a bad flight. He'd panicked and gone down on the 'plane, so had had to be doped and as a result he didn't feel very sociable when he arrived at the Hartingtons' Yorkshire home in mid-winter. As he only had a New Zealand summer coat, the weather was a terrible shock for him and he was horrified by the snow. Amanda found him trying to stick his head in a stone wall to get away from it!

Amanda did quite a lot of Jaybee's early fittening work in 1998. I ran him *hors concours* in a few intermediate classes to try and get to know him but was a bit disconcerted at Belton when a New Zealand rider, seeing me on Jaybee, said, 'Oh yes, we looked at him but we thought he was a nappy little bugger!' However, Jaybee seemed to go well for me and I ran him in an advanced class at Bishop Burton, where he went clear, to qualify him for Bramham.

The going at Bramham was bottomless that year and it was very wet with torrential rain on cross-country day. We were lying third after dressage, but the steeplechase track was in such a state that I was considering pulling out. However, Jaybee didn't seem to mind it and

above: Congratulations from Ceci Vestey after our trail-blazing cross-country ride at Badminton

opposite: Despite his inexperience, Jaybee looks the part over the Footbridge

Alex.

ploughed on, getting sixteen time faults, and then trotted happily around Phase C. Giles Rowsell, our then chairman of selectors, and Mike Tucker advised me that the riders who were taking the long routes on the cross-country were sliding around, but the direct ones seemed to be jumping all right. I followed this advice and Jaybee gave me a great ride, going clear although with a quite a few time faults. Next day he showjumped clear, which was nice after our Puhinui debacle, and this pulled us up to 14th place and reaffirmed my belief that I had brought a good horse back.

We did one more one-day event and then went to Boekelo, but it was a wash-out in the pouring rain which by then seemed to be the hallmark of 1998 and the organisers turned it into a CIC instead (international one-day event). Jaybee had done a good dressage but then at probably the easiest fence on the course, a logpile and hedge, he put his feet on the top and jumped me off. I landed on his head before I hit the ground and broke a rib. I was in absolute agony, but I still had Rangitoto to ride, so I kept very quiet about that as I didn't want to be stopped from riding!

Next year I felt that Jaybee might be too inexperienced for Badminton, but I entered him anyway and after he went well in the advanced classes at Belton and Witton Castle I decided to go for it. However, when the draw was announced (which was while I was away riding The Moose in Lexington in the USA) I discovered that we had been picked first to go. I felt as sick as a parrot. I don't usually mind going first because then you don't have anyone else's problems to worry about, but I did feel unsure about it on such a young horse. However, it turned out to be a blessing in disguise.

I was really pleased with his dressage, which put us into fourth place behind Mark Todd on none other than Broadcast News, who was nearly twice Jaybee's age! The commentator Sally O'Connor was very complimentary. She said, 'As a youngster Jaybee lacked the strength to really get off the ground, but his movement was so elastic and relaxed and his walk was excellent.'

We certainly had the best of the going on the cross-country as it was a horrendously wet day and it had rained overnight on the course too. There was a lot of nervousness anyway about the fact that there were so many twists and turns which were made worse by the tightness of the roping, and some riders were very outspoken in their criticism of the designer Hugh Thomas, both in the papers and on television. All of this, combined with the weather and an unpopular new scoring system which has now been dropped, did create unfortunate controversy for what was Badminton's 50th birthday and should have been a great anniversary.

Jaybee started out a little green, but I was thrilled at how well he was

galloping and jumping by the end. He always seemed to find an extra leg, especially at the Beaufort Staircase where he scrambled over the log pile at the top, but by the end he was jumping really confidently and he finished very well. As the day went on I couldn't believe that no one else had overtaken us on the leaderboard, as we had twenty-six time faults. Amazingly this was to be the joint fastest time of the day along with Austin O'Connor on Simply Rhett.

The new experimental scoring system, in which there were no divisions or coefficients in the marking, was designed to simplify matters for the public and

opposite: Victory lap of honour, Badminton 1999

'Everyone kept telling me I had it in the bag, but I was still incredibly nervous ... Supposing I lost my way or fell off or had five fences down!'

above: Photo call at Beamsley for Jaybee and his trophies

take the complicated maths out of it, but many people felt that it caused problems with riders clocking up cricket scores on the cross-country and becoming dissuaded from carrying on. They also feel it affected the relative influences of the phases and reduced the importance of the showjumping. This system was dropped at the end of the year after riders voted overwhelmingly to revert to the traditional system, but at Badminton 1999 it meant that I was left with an amazing four showjumps in hand over Toddy on Word For Word instead of what would have been one under the usual system.

Everyone kept telling me I had it in the bag, but I was still incredibly nervous, as previous showjumping disasters are always on your mind. Supposing I lost my way or fell off or had five fences down! Ken Clawson, who trains the British team in showjumping, was a great help to me beforehand and, of course, Jenny was there too trying to keep me calm. Jaybee did have one fence down; I probably overrode him at the water ditch to prevent him spooking and after he'd made a huge leap over that he ran on and then hit the next. However, we would still have won under the old system. And, despite the fact that everyone said that it wouldn't be exciting and that I had the competition won beforehand, the crowd was fantastic. The parade of competitors earlier in the day is always a wonderful atmosphere, with lots of cheering, and they really were brilliant on this afternoon, which made it very special.

The summer preparation for the European Championships at Luhmühlen in Germany did not quite go according to plan and there was a definite panic that Jaybee was short on cross-country runs. He didn't get his run at Auchinleck, because I had fallen off A Mouse Called Mickey, but he did get his run in the CIC at Thirlestane. Ironically that was because his dressage wasn't good enough to be in the top ten who didn't run due to Polly Phillipps's fatal fall. So Thirlestane was his only cross-country run that summer, but it is a big course and he made it feel easy, which was a relief as you never know how a horse will come out of their first Badminton.

Some of the team riders, including myself, wanted to ride at Blenheim, which was the weekend before Luhmühlen, so it was decided that we would take the team horses and have team concentration there. This did not suit Jaybee at all; he was completely wired to the moon as he couldn't understand why he was at a three-day event and not running across country.

By the time we got to Luhmühlen he was totally confused and thought that he must have had his three-day run, so his dressage was rather switched off. His trot work had improved since Badminton, but his canter work had deteriorated, possibly because the concentrated training had tired his back muscles. He is not keen on too much dressage and, being bored, did not get as good a mark as he might have done.

No one was keen to go first for the team. I had offered, but was asked to go last, and the task fell to Jeanette Brakewell, who did a great job on her team debut. When it came to my turn, I was told to have a clear round, preferably in the time, but that I could have a few time faults! We knew it was possible to make the time, even doing the long route at both water complexes, which were team orders but with which I was in full agreement. I knew it would make me down on time, but there was every opportunity to make it up later.

'Team concentration did not suit Jaybee at all; he was completely wired to the moon ...'

Phase A went past the dressage arena and Jaybee was so horrified at the thought that he might have to do some more dressage that he went into a sulk and I had to kick him. I really thought he was ill, but as soon as he saw the steeplechase he was like a raging bull with excitement.

I now realise that he is a very laid-back horse at three-day events; after the trot-up he will go back to sleep in his box as if to conserve energy. He looks green at the start of the cross-country, but I now know that he is just sleepy and I will probably have to warm him up more in future.

The closed-circuit TV of the cross-country at Luhmühlen was not all that comprehensive so we were grateful for Lucinda Green's information from the farmyard complex on the far side of the course. She advised me to go for two short strides to the first spread, two attacking strides to the next, three long ones to the corner and then three to the huge table on a right-hand turn. These turned out to be long distances for a little horse like Jaybee and, although I was not aware of any problems, being so focused on keeping going, it so happened that most of the equestrian press would happen to be there to witness a rather untidy scramble with Jaybee kicking out a flag at the corner. The table on the turn really was vast; had it been on a straight line I think there would have been some nasty falls there, but as there was a turn to set horses up, it jumped well.

By this stage we were about ten or fifteen seconds down on the clock, but the last part of the course was through twisting woods so I let him have a longer rein and he balanced himself and really scooted around the bends. We finished exactly on the button, which was a great feeling as, after all these years, it was actually the first time I have done it. Planned of course!

Tina Gifford and Pippa Funnell, numbers two and three for the team, had gone really well too and we were in the lead by miles in the showjumping after the Swedish team dropped down, having lost a horse in the last inspection. Jaybee was not as sparky as he might have been and, in hindsight, I think a lack of previous cross-country runs was the problem, but he only had one down and finished fifth. I was thrilled with him and felt this had really confirmed him as a particularly special horse.

Winning this team gold was also a very special result. The team was under enormous pressure to qualify for the Sydney Olympics, having lost the qualification when Coral Cove was disqualified from the previous year's World Games (see page 116). I hadn't really thought much about Sydney beforehand but then the press kept ringing up and asking if I felt under pressure and so I started to think that perhaps I did!

(see page 116)

opposite:
Coming in from the steeplechase at Luhmühlen

below: The winning team: Tina Gifford, Pippa Funnell, Jeanette Brakewell and me

'Winning this team gold was also a very special result. The team was under enormous pressure ...'

It was a particularly good team atmosphere at this championships, very relaxed but very positive and with no 'prima donnas'. Chris Bartle was a great success as team manager and he worked well with his assistant Mike Kingscote and with Mandy Stibbe, who had stepped in as chairman of selectors when Giles Rowsell resigned. It was a particular triumph both for Pippa Funnell, who really deserved to win the individual title, and also for Mandy, as the usual suspects kept telling her that she had picked the wrong team. It's always great when you stuff the critics!

a great trier
Rangitoto

Rangitoto, my third Kiwi purchase, was named after an uninhabited volcanic island off Auckland. Blyth Tait, the World and Olympic champion, had brought him over as a novice and produced him to two-star level.

above: Rangitoto clears the GNER train at Bramham 1999

opposite: Our first outing together at Thirlestane, where we finished third

'Blyth also said, "You'll hate his dressage and I have to warn you that he'll never do a medium trot" …'

Blyth suggested that I might like to look at his youngsters with a view to buying one and he thought I'd particularly like Rangitoto. However, Blyth also said, 'You'll hate his dressage and I have to warn you that he'll never do medium trot!' But when I went to see Rangitoto, I didn't dislike him on the flat and so decided to return with the Vesteys in tow. Ceci liked him too, and so we bought him.

Rangitoto has taken a while to sort out on the flat, but he is a very trainable and honest horse who will bust a gut to do what you want. He is also quite strong. On our first outing, at Thirlestane Castle in the summer of 1998, although we finished third there were at least three fences where I don't mind admitting that everything was in the wrong place and my reins were everywhere. However, that autumn I took him to Boekelo and, despite the pain of my broken rib from the earlier fall on Jaybee, I was pleased with the confident cross-country ride that he gave me to finish 20th.

Our first three-day run, at Bramham in 1999, was rather memorable for unfortunate reasons. By this time members of the British Horse Trials Association were making it clear that they had had enough of the way the Coral Cove case had been handled. [Coral Cove was Polly Phillipps's British team horse in 1998 who failed a dope test at the World Games and subsequently got the British team eliminated. As a result, Britain lost the bronze medal and was not qualified for the Sydney Olympics.] The event kicked off with a very acrimonious and aggressive members' meeting (they are usually very sedate, even dull, affairs) and the following day the team manager Giles Rowsell and vet Andy Bathe, both of whom we felt had done a very good job – team management

had never been so open and so popular with riders before they came – resigned. Polly herself was riding at Bramham – in fact she finished second on Coral Cove – and the whole atmosphere became most uncomfortable and very much overshadowed the actual competition.

As far as Rangitoto was concerned, I was very pleased with him. His dressage had improved by about twenty marks and he gave me a brave, but not too strong, cross-country ride. We incurred fifty-two time penalties, which lost us our seventh placing after the dressage, but I wasn't too concerned. We lost time because I had to set him up for fences as I felt he was too much on the forehand and I couldn't let him run on. But he only had one showjump down next day and I went home pleased.

I decided not to enter him for Burghley, as I felt he was too green a galloper, so instead I entered him for Blenheim. I was very taken aback to get a dressage mark of 103 (under the experimental system) as I really felt that he had improved,

'The whole atmosphere became most uncomfortable and very much overshadowed the actual competition ...'

but we had a good cross-country round. It was the first time I had pushed him for the time but we nearly blew it at the double of corners at the end. It was my fault as he was galloping a bit freely and when I said to him 'There's the spot [to take off]' nothing happened. He shot to the left and took out the flags but was then incredibly honest and squeezed himself over the second corner. A lot of horses could have said 'You must be joking' and run out.

Next day we had one fence down and five time penalties which was caused by my suddenly having a panic about the route. I just couldn't remember if I was meant to turn left or right, dithered and wasted time. But it was a good enough performance to qualify us for Badminton, which meant Rangitoto could be added to the list of possibles for Sydney.

Rangitoto is a great cross-country horse and, therefore, would be a good team horse, but I don't know if his dressage will ever be good enough for individual honours. He isn't very good at concentrating and so the quality of his work varies.

'... and when I said to him "There's the spot [to take off]" nothing happened'

above: On our way to an advanced win at Chatsworth

opposite: Jumping cleanly into the Kidney Pond at Bramham

a Mouse Called
Mickey

'So ugly that only his mother
could love him ...'

below: *With owner Lady Hartington*

A Mouse Called Mickey was yet another Bryce Newman purchase.
I went to see him in New Zealand in December 1998 the day after a
couple of Kiwi riders had been through Bryce's youngsters – and left
Mickey behind! And Bryce himself described Mickey as, 'So ugly
that only a mother could love him'! But I loved his expression, even
though his big plain head seemed to be upside down on his neck
and he didn't have a decent trot. He had raced as a two- and three-
year-old, had been bought as a showjumper, and Bryce had just got
him to intermediate eventing level.

I have never been very keen on black horses (even preferring
chestnut mares!) but Bryce had insisted that Mickey was brown.
However, when I asked why he was called Mickey Mouse, Bryce
accidentally replied, 'Because he's black!'

I took him cross-country schooling and liked him. He failed
the vet first time, due to a splint, but passed second time around
and I managed to persuade Amanda Hartington to buy him to add
to her collection. He came over to her home for the winter, where
she always likes to ride her horses, but he bucked her off first time!

Mickey's first event was a novice at Brougham, in Cumbria,
where I ran him *hors concours* and he went clear. He was then fourth
in an intermediate at Witton Castle and won at Belton.

His first three-day event, Compiègne in France, was a big
step up for him. It was on the weekend after Badminton and I was
still on a high so was really pleased when we finished eighth and
best of the British. Compiègne turned into rather a dressage
competition and it was difficult to make up any placings
afterwards. Mickey is another horse who has little understanding
of medium trot and I have to say that our test was pretty basic,
but, nonetheless, we finished on that score and I felt that Mickey
was showing potential.

A couple of months later we went to a one-day event at
Castletown where he was much better on the flat and we finished
second. I then took him to do the advanced at Auchinleck, where
he did a presentable dressage and even showed some medium trot.
He showjumped clear too, but then I fell off him across country.
He got in too deep to a cross-country fence and jumped very big
with his backside up in the air; I was hanging off one side, so he
got fed up with me and bucked me off. We banged heads and I
ended up with a very bloody broken nose!

I took him to Blair Castle, but he was lame in the dressage due
to a bruised foot so, after a one-day run at Aske Hall I took him to
Boekelo ten days later. Mickey had only started to think about
flying changes the week before, so it goes without saying that his

above: The winning
British team at
Compiègne: Chris
Hunnable, Katie
Parker, and me with
our chef d'équipe
Bridget Parker

'I ended up hanging off one side, so he
got fed up with me and bucked me
off. We banged heads and I ended up
with a very bloody broken nose ...'

test at Boekelo was very green with only a vaguely recognisable extended trot. But when I saw the video later, I realised that he has got it all there to come.

It rained, which made the cross-country sticky, so I took him steadily on the steeplechase. He started jumping the fences very big, but as we went on he understood that he didn't have to jump these fences so high. I took my watch off and decided to ride the cross-country according to how he felt. In fact, he coped very well with the ground and built up speed so that by the end he was flying; it was the perfect learning curve. We just had one very scary moment, at a double of pimples. He jumped on and off the first one, which had a stride distance on the top, perfectly well, but he got confused by the second, smaller, one and never really took off. He basically skidded across it on his shoulder and it was only self-preservation that kept him upright, but the crowd cheered madly and somehow we all stayed in one piece.

Next day his showjumping was very good; he went clear and we finished 14th, which, like Rangitoto, elevated him to the status of Olympic possibility.

whatever next...?

My background in eventing probably differs somewhat from some of my contemporaries in the sport in that I was basically self-taught. Jenny's mother, who ran a riding school which her sister now runs, was probably the first person who ever gave me any formal tuition.

Then, when I first had Sir Wattie, I used to go to Barbara Slane-Fleming, who helped me enormously and who still comes to me now if I have a problem. I never had a single jumping lesson until I was on the team for the Los Angeles Olympics, when I was helped by Pat Burgess.

Much later when, thanks to riding some 'iffy' showjumpers, I lost confidence in myself, I went to Lars Sederholm, who trained countless event riders of the past when he was at Waterstock. Lars completely restored my confidence; he doesn't use any gimmicks, he is just a very sound person who understands horses and is quite a psychologist.

Team preparation has changed almost out of all recognition since I was a newcomer in 1984 and this is very much thanks to the Lottery funding which has come to the sport for team training, and which has meant that as 'élite' riders we have to have regular dealings with people like nutritionists and psychologists.

We have had team talks from a sports psychologist, which I tend to find rather squirm-making and obvious – instructions like if you don't concentrate, you won't win and you have to look after number one in order to focus your energy – but it is quite uncomfortable being confronted with these home truths.

It's amazing how many sportsmen use a psychologist nowadays, but I have always found that Jenny fulfils that role for me better than anyone else could. After more than twenty years of marriage she knows me better than anybody, she understands my moods, she knows instinctively what is worrying me and I owe her a enormous amount for her organisation and support over the years.

'… many sportsmen use a psychologist nowadays, but Jenny fulfils that role for me better than anyone else could'

Yes! I do do some of the dirty work sometimes …!

However, I have found the nutritionists' advice helpful. A few years ago I had a thyroid problem and put on quite a bit of weight. I was about to run the London marathon and had been training, but a bad fall in the Cheltenham Foxhunters on the Stevensons' Randolph Place put paid to that and afterwards my thyroid went haywire. I now take my diet seriously – I lost a stone in a month over the winter of 1999 thanks to a cabbage soup diet! – and run every day, which I enjoy. It's proved a huge bonus in that I don't feel at all tired at the end of a three-day event.

Veterinary monitoring has also developed out of all recognition and is all part of team selection. New technology has meant that horses' leg problems show up even before they have become a real concern and, indeed, the odd shadow on a leg does not necessarily mean that the horse will go lame. These developments have meant that horses who would previously have been passed sound to compete have not been able to be selected, which has caused the selectors quite a headache. Obviously, you cannot take a horse who has a question mark over his soundness to a championships, even though he may appear perfectly alright. This extra knowledge has to be a good thing, but I would be sorry to see vets relying totally on technology and losing the judgement of sight and feel.

'The down side is that as such a senior rider you are expected to have a point of view on everything ...'

above & opposite:
Dealing with the press and public is all part of the job

I still love the sport, but inevitably with success and seniority – I am ten or more years older than most of the top British riders – does come a certain amount of hassle which tends to get in the way of competing. I don't wish to sound ungrateful at some of the attention, because much of it comes with great goodwill and not only is of personal benefit, but is also good for the sport. I am not, however, a good committee person and the down side is that as a senior rider you are expected to have a point of view on everything, which can be wearying. After the tragic run of rider deaths in 1999 I did seventeen interviews in one day at Blenheim and that was in between trying to compete and set off for the European Championships in Germany. That year was a difficult period for the sport anyway, what with the much-publicised Coral Cove doping case and then the terrible run of fatal accidents and, on looking back, I realise that these background worries probably did detract from my performances at some events. Obviously all riders make mistakes, but we don't expect to pay for them with our lives.

People often ask me what changes I would like to see in the format of the sport, as there are continual calls to abandon or shorten certain phases or alter the order of phases. While the welfare of the horse coupled with horse and rider safety have to come first, I am also a traditionalist. I adore the sport as it is – that is why I wanted to do it at the age of eighteen and I haven't changed my views. The three-day event is designed to produce the all-round horse and cutting out the stamina test would ruin that.

If I get to the Sydney Olympics, it will probably be my last team competition. It is a fantastic honour to ride for your country and I have been fortunate to experience it more than most, but perhaps I am getting too old for some of the fuss!

As long as I have this wonderful string of horses and two such terrific owners, I fully intend to continue to compete at the big events and it is only later on that I plan to settle for bringing on novices. I haven't any definite plans for the future – in fact, I'm open to offers!

stable notes

SIR WATTIE

Stable name: Wattie

Career highlights: 1983 1st Bramham
1984 6th Badminton
1985 team gold and individual silver
European chamionships
1986 1st Badminton
1987 team gold European
championships
1988 1st Badminton, team and
invidual silver Seoul Olympics

Born: 1976
Breeding: By Bronze Hill (TB) out of
Rosa (half Welsh cob)
Owners: Dame Jean Maxwell-Scott
and Susan Luczyc-Wynowska (his
breeders) and The Edinburgh Woollen
Mill
Height: 16.2hh
Colour: Bay
Talents: Consistency. Won more
events than any other of my horses
Likes: Getting home – he always
whinnied when the lorry neared home
Dislikes: Would sulk if not exercised
first thing in the morning

OXFORD BLUE

Stable name: Robbie

Career highlights: 1984 3rd Badminton;
team silver Los Angeles Olympics
1985 team gold and individual bronze
European Championships
1986 team gold World Championships

Born: 1976
Breeding: TB, by Cagirana out of
Blewberry Fair
Owner: Elizabeth Davidson
Height: 16.2hh
Colour: Brown
Talents: Very fast! Laid-back
temperament – our first groom,
George, learnt to ride on him
Weaknesses: Showjumping

STANWICK GHOST

Stable name: Jack

Career highlights: 1992 1st Scottish
Novice Championships; 4th Blair
Castle CCI**

1993 2nd Saumur CCI***; 4th
Blenheim CCI***
1994 8th Punchestown CCI***
1996 6th Badminton CCI**** (cross-
country leader); member of British
Olympic team
1997 13th Badminton CCI**** (cross-
country leader)
1999 1st Chatsworth CIC***

Born: 1986
Breeding: TB, by Grey Ghost out of
Stanwick Gold. Bred by Miss Sally
Williamson
Owner: Lady Hartington
Height: 16.2hh
Colour: Grey
Talents: Fantastic dressage, foot-
perfect cross-country. Natural poser
Weaknesses: Drooping legs over
showjumps, never won a three-day
event despite leading after the
dressage and cross-country
Likes: Food, showing off, getting
dirty, lots of attention, biting people
Dislikes: Dieting, hard work, having
rugs and girths done up, being caught
in the field

GLENBURNIE

Stable name: Glen

Career highlights: 1986 4th
Burghley
1988 2nd Badminton
1989 team gold European
Championships
1991 team and individual gold
European Championships
Competed at five Badmintons

Born: 1978
Breeding: TB by Precipice Wood out
of Mayday, bred by Capt The Hon and
Mrs Gerald Maitland-Carew
Owner: The Edinburgh Woollen Mill
Height: 16.3hh
Colour: Grey
Talents: Incredible speed and scope.
Weaknesses: Very strong, if not
slightly mad, across country; grumpy
in the stable and usually kicked
someone in the 10-minute box!
Liked: Galloping and hunting
Disliked: Dressage and idiots

MURPHY HIMSELF

Stable name: Murphy

Career highlights: 1984 1st
Avenches (with Ginny Leng)
1986 1st Le Touquet CCI; 1st Burghley
(both with Ginny Leng)
1988 1st Boekelo
1990 team and individual silver
Stockholm World Games
1991 2nd Badminton
1992 member of British Olympic team

Born: 1978
Breeding: Irish-bred, by Royal
Renown
Owner: The Edinburgh Woollen Mill
Height: 16.1½hh
Colour: Grey
Talents: Incredible scope
Weaknesses: Out of control!
Liked: Taking off, especially on the
way to the gallops. Making horrible
faces. Being in the limelight
Disliked: Being bullied in the field —
he was a real wimp

ARAKAI

Stable name: Harry

Career highlights: 1994 1st Puhinui
CCI* (with producer Gee Davidson)
1995 10th Taupo CCI** (with Vaughn
Jefferis)
1996 21st Boekelo CCI***
1997 14th Badminton CCI****; 10th
and team gold Burghley European
1999 1st advanced Auchinlec; 6th
after cross-country at Burghley
CCI****
Born: 1988
Breeding: NZ TB, by Ring The Bell out
of Happy Hostess
Owner: Lady Vestey
Height: 17hh
Colour: Bay
Talents: Amazing natural ability
across country and showjumping,
bold, scopey, quick-thinking and has a
big stride which covers the ground
Weaknesses: Inability to stay cool
and calm, worries about competitions
until he is there, difficulty in keeping
consistent weight

Likes: Jumping and galloping, going to competitions, companionship
Dislikes: Having mane and tail pulled, being alone

JAYBEE

Stable name: JB

Career highlights: 1997 9th Puhinui CCI***
1998 2nd Floors Castle OI (first ever run in Britain); 14th Bramham CCI***
1999 1st Badminton CCI**** (youngest horse for 28 years); 5th and team gold Luhmühlen Europeans

Born: 1990
Breeding: NZ TB by Norfolk Air (GB)
Owner: Lady Hartington
Height: 16.1hh
Colour: Brown
Talents: Uncomplicated in all three phases, athletic both on the flat and jumping, precise and big-thinking for a little horse
Weaknesses: Can be lazy, doesn't like being hassled
Likes: Jumping big and technical fences, bucking people off, staying out in the field, his friend the goose
Dislikes: Other horses being ridden first, being confined in small places

RANGITOTO

Stable name: Thomas

Career highlights: 1998 placed Lille

and Windsor three-day events (with Blyth Tait)
1998 3rd Thirlestane advanced; 17th Boekelo CIC***
1999 1st advanced Chatsworth; 2nd advanced Thirlestane Castle; 20th Blenheim CCI***

Born: 1990
Breeding: NZ TB by Jigg's Alarm
Owner: Lady Vestey
Height: 16.2hh
Colour: Grey
Talents: Accurate across country, careful showjumper
Weaknesses: Dressage has taken time
Likes: Speed, untying complicated knots, being bathed
Dislikes: Contact with other horses

A MOUSE CALLED MICKEY

Stable name: Mickey

Career highlights: 1999 8th Compiègne CCI**; 14th Boekelo CCI***

Born: 1991
Breeding: NZ TB by Zepher Vescent
Owner: Lady Hartington
Talents: Finds showjumping easy, sharp thinker, athletic and bold
Weaknesses: Flatwork (he is still learning), finds it hard to use of his neck muscles correctly
Likes: Bucking, keeping people on their toes, one-to-one attention
Dislikes: Being clipped

PICTURE ACKNOWLEDGEMENTS
All photographs by Kit Houghton except the following:
Lady Hartington's collection pp4-5, 14(top & btm), 15, 84-85, 86(left), 92(left & right), 106 (btm), 115, 120, 122 and 128; Eric Bryce p8(btm); Mrs Susan Luczycwyhowska p16(top); Hugo M Czerny pp16(btm), 22, 28, 36 and 54-55; Equestrian Services Thorney pp20(top) and 101; Shaw-Shot Photography p27; Trevor Meeks p43; Capital Press p44; Alan Johnson p46(top); Stuart Newsham p46(btm); The Advertiser pp48-49; Findlay Davidson p50; Reinhard Koblitz p64; Nick Gill pp82(btm), 86(right) and 124; Helen Revington p95; Ray Kennedy Photography pp96-97; Action Images p100(btm); Paul L E Raper-Züllig p108; Alex Colquhoun p109; Richard Clive Photography p113(left & right); Morris Photography Ltd pp116 and 118; Stark's collection pp37(top), 47, 61, 82(top) and 119

A DAVID & CHARLES BOOK

Publisher: Pippa Rubinstein
Commissioning editor: Sue Viccars
Designer: Les Dominey
Art editor: Sue Cleave
Production: Beverley Richardson

First published in the UK in 2000

Copyright © Kate Green 2000

Kate Green has asserted her right to be identified as author of this work in accordance with the Copyright, Designs and Patents Act, 1988.

A catalogue record for this book is available from the British Library.

ISBN 0 7153 1071 2

Colour origination by Global Colour Ltd
Printed in Hong Kong
by Dai Nippon Co.
for David & Charles
Brunel House   Newton Abbot   Devon